# THE
# ORGANISED
# BUSINESS

How to free yourself from your business,
*maximise* its profits and make
it run like clockwork

**William H. A. Wood**

**The Organised Business**

Copyright © 2014 William H. A. Wood

www.theorganisedbusiness.co.uk

ISBN 978-1-907308-33-8

First published in Great Britain in 2014 by Compass Publishing.

Set by The Book Refinery Ltd.

Printed in the United Kingdom by Berforts Information Press.

## Dedicated to David Wood

*1944 – 2010*

Without you, none of this would have been possible.

Also dedicated to all the big and little Woods
wherever you are.

# Contents

# Contents

# Introduction

*"Anxiety is caused by lack of control, organization, preparation, and action."*
**David Kekich**

If you are reading this book you are, more than likely, a business owner or about to become one. As a business owner myself, I have some questions for you. These are mostly rhetorical and designed to make you think about your business and its role in your life.

## Do You Feel in Control of Your Business?

- ✓ Do you feel you have your finger on the pulse of all aspects of your business?
- ✓ Does your business run like clockwork?
- ✓ Is your business doing what you want it to do?
- ✓ Is your role in the business what you want it to be?
- ✓ Are you doing the tasks you want to be doing?
- ✓ Does your business add value to your life?
- ✓ Do you feel you spend too much time working in your business and not enough time on it?
- ✓ Do you feel that you are always working but never getting enough done?
- ✓ Is your business detracting from your life and making you or your family unhappy?

If you swayed toward the negative when answering these questions, then this book is for you. If you feel out of control, or are unhappy with the results of your business or the effect it has on your life, then read on.

I wrote this book for small business owners who feel their businesses have massive potential – if only they could get it, and themselves organised.

Small business owners are, in my humble opinion, the backbone of this country, in fact of any country. I am talking about the types of people who work in their businesses for six or seven days a week, and then go home to do a bit more just to keep on top of all the work. They represent hard work, determination and the will to succeed, and they are what make this country great.

I am not just saying this because this is who the book is aimed at; I am saying it because I truly believe it!

My mother and father were small business owners, and they worked extremely hard. They managed to raise three children and grow a business, whilst moving us from a council estate in South Wales to a place where we could get a decent education. I have the utmost respect for them, and for anyone who dares to step out from being a wage slave to start their own business.

So why is it that one small business owner can appear to be more successful than another one? I know for a fact that it isn't because one works harder than the other.

The answer is, as you would expect, complex and varied. It could be that they are simply in the wrong business or have a bad product or service. That aside, there are many examples of businesses in the same industry where one is successful, and one isn't.

*In this scenario, a big part of the problem simply comes down to how organised the owner is.*

### Real Life Example

Many of my clients are electrical contractors, and I know how difficult that industry can be. I have seen one fail spectacularly, one fail over and over again, one that is not growing and has chosen to stay as a one-man band, and one that is thriving, but the owner is very stressed.

The work these businesses do is essentially the same, but they achieve very different results. I'm not going to use the one-man band as an example, because for the purposes of this book he doesn't really have a business as such. The only real differences between the others, are the individuals running the businesses, and how they organise and plan them.

### The business that keeps failing

The business that keeps failing is in that situation because it is doing the same thing over and over again and achieving the same results. The repeated failures come down to a few things, including a lack of planning, lack of systems and ultimately the failure to work on the business.

### The business that is thriving

The business that is thriving is costing the owner personally because he is working a hundred hours a week just to keep it going – but it is going and growing. The question is; how long can a business that relies on its owner in this way survive if he doesn't figure out a way for it to continue to operate when he is removed from the scenario?

That aside, he is extremely organised and makes sure things are delivered on time and on budget. He keeps his customers, staff and suppliers happy.

*Does any of this sound familiar to you?*

An organised business has much more chance of being successful than a disorganised one, and how organised the business is, ultimately comes down to *how organised the owner is.*

**Think about that for a minute:**

>   *An organised business owner = an organised business.*

>   *An organised business = a more successful business.*

## Why I Wrote This Book

Over the last 15 years I have helped small businesses achieve their aims, and I have seen how incredibly difficult it can be to run a business. I have also listened to what business owners have said to me during this time, and have learnt what works and what doesn't when it comes to growing a business.

Ultimately, the respect for my target audience drove me to want to share what I have learnt, and through this book I would like to share this information with you. On numerous occasions, clients have told me that if only they had known what I know, their lives and businesses would have been much better, and my aim with this book is to help make your business life easier and give you more of a chance of success.

Along the way, I will impart the classic mistakes that owners make, why they are made and how to avoid them.

This book is both for those just starting out and experienced business owners who just can't seem to make it work. I hope you enjoy it.

### How to use this book

I will outline the key concepts and give you practical advice on how to organise your business.

To illustrate each piece of advice given in the chapter, I will use an example called *'The Tale of Two Brothers'*, which is based around the real-life experiences of clients of mine. These small business owners are brothers called Stephen and John, who both learnt their trade by working in their father's business, and if they had lived in the same part of the country they probably would have gone into business together, but as they didn't, they started up the same type of businesses, but in different locations.

Stephen is super organised, uses all the techniques in this book and has a successful, well run business. His life is busy but not hectic.

The opposite is true for John, who is the person I targeted this book at. His life is busy, hectic and stressful!

## The chapters explained

With the exception of Chapters 1 and 2, you don't have to read or action these chapters in order; you just have to read and action them all *at some point.*

### Chapter 1: Why Get Organised?

In this chapter, using the two businesses described above, I will give you some real-life examples of why it is so important to organise.

There is more than one way of getting things done. Some can make your life harder and some easier, some can mean your business will succeed, and some can contribute to it failing or, at best, remaining static. Sometimes it's easy to be too close to the business to see there are better ways of doing things.

### Chapter 2: Organise Your Planning

*'If you fail to plan – you plan to fail.'* This old saying has a lot of truth in it; planning doesn't just happen, you have to organise and make time to plan.

In this chapter, we discuss why it's critical to plan and why more businesses don't. I will also go through a planning technique that really works for many business owners.

### Chapter 3: Organise Your Systems

A major part of running an organised business is down to the use of systems, i.e. the internal processes that successful businesses have in place. Some businesses will have really thought about these and mapped them out, whereas others will have just let them develop organically. This chapter is organised into two parts. *Part 1* sets out how to write and develop your systems with a proven method I have used for many businesses.

*Part 2* shares with you how to implement these systems into your business.

This chapter demonstrates how you can use systems and processes in your business to get *real control* of it.

### Chapter 4: Organise Your Computer

If your PC, Mac or Cloud storage account is a mess (with things filed everywhere so you can never find anything when you need it) I will show you some practical solutions on how to organise it so you can find files fast and efficiently.

### Chapter 5: Organise Your Sales And Marketing

Sales and marketing don't just happen; you have to have an organised, methodical and dogged approach. In this chapter, we review the approaches needed to get this vital part of your business organised.

### Chapter 6: Organise Your Finances

Many small business owners don't understand their accounts, and only keep their books for the VAT man and accountant. Here, we look at some simple things you can do to get on top of your finances and take control of your business.

On the Television Programme, '*Dragon's Den*', there is a very good reason that the prospective entrepreneurs are always asked about their finances, and that is because these numbers are vital to their business. Understanding your own finances will really help you clarify how your business is doing, where you can make improvements, and how to get ahead of your competitors!

I will show you some techniques and tools that will help you produce a set of books that will help you make decisions based on actual figures, and not just on gut feeling. This chapter is broken into two parts. *Part 1* introduces you to the information you need to know for basic accounting, and *Part 2* delves a little bit deeper for those who want to get a fuller understanding of the concepts.

### Chapter 7: Organise Your Cash

This chapter gives some practical advice on how to make sure you don't run out of cash. Cash to your business is like the air that you breathe – without it you won't survive for long.

### Chapter 8: Organise Your Paperwork

Do you want to hear a joke?  The paperless office!

As yet it hasn't happened and is unlikely to in my lifetime. Less paper maybe, but paper is here to stay – so get yours organised. This chapter explains how.

### Chapter 9: Organise Yourself

Your business is ultimately a reflection of you. If you are organised, your business will be too. This chapter examines some strategies to help you be more organised.

## Pen to paper, or fingers to keyboard

I'm also going to ask you to do some exercises called *'Don't just read it, do it!'* throughout the book, with some *very* specific guidance to help you overcome the issues that could be holding you back.

To help you through these exercises and to ensure you actually implement my call to actions, I have developed a workbook to go along with the book. This is **FREE** and can be downloaded **from book.theorganisedbusiness.co.uk (no www needed)**

The workbook contains *all the actions and exercises* listed in this book and provides space for you to complete them.

Also on the website there are other **RESOURCES,** which will be mentioned throughout the book. These are also available **FREE** to all readers and are designed to help you in your journey to becoming an organised business.

So, just visit book.theorganisedbusiness.co.uk and download the workbook, it really will help you implement all of my suggestions!

*So with all that said...*

# Chapter 1: Why Get Organised?

*"To be in hell is to drift; to be in heaven is to steer."*
**George Bernard Shaw**

Running a business is difficult enough even when you are organised, but if you aren't – good luck!

As a business owner, sometimes it can feel that not only are you trying to juggle too many balls, but you're also spinning plates and riding a unicycle at the same time. If you're not organised enough to cope with the circus skills required, then eventually you will drop a ball, a plate or even worse come crashing down off the unicycle.

However, in my view, a lack of organisation is worse than just dropping a ball, because a dropped ball every now and then isn't the end of the world, but a full blown catastrophe is a reflection of your business, and of course will determine your business's success or failure.

Simply put, *the more organised you are, the more successful you will be.*

What's more, even if you are successfully on top of your circus tricks and your business is growing, then you're more than likely going to limit that growth because your ability to juggle is not endless, and time is not on your side.

Eventually, you will have to step down, for whatever reason, and hand over the business, but if it's not in a state to be handed over, then all that hard work will have been for nothing.

We all know the failure rate statistics for small business owners, and needless to say, they are unacceptably high.

If your business is in the small percentage that makes it through the first three years and you aren't organised, then your chances of going on to real success are virtually none. This is because as you scale the business, inevitably you will need to hire more staff to cope with the extra work, invoicing, purchases and marketing etc. If your business doesn't have organised systems in place for coping, it will implode under the pressure.

*Without systems and organisation you*
*cannot scale a business.*

## Scaling can be defined as:

A characteristic of a system, model or function (or business) that describes its capability to cope and perform under an increased or expanding workload. A system (or business) that scales well will be able to maintain or even increase its level of performance or efficiency when tested by larger operational demands.

So if you are seriously thinking about growth, you need to get organised and get some systems in place.

### A Quick Note on Scalability

As you go through this book and start implementing the actions within, it's worth noting that any organisation, systems, processes or tools that you put into place must be scalable. The system you put in place should have the ability to expand as the business grows.

For example, a client of mine was very pleased with the purchase of a new whiteboard. It worked well on some levels; recording all jobs in progress, it was easy to understand, but it was also high maintenance, in that you had to virtually re-write it every time it needed to be updated

What they hadn't considered was that it wasn't scalable. If they achieved success and needed to double the amount of content on it, they would have to purchase another board each time they expanded. Eventually they would have run out of wall space for all the whiteboards.

 **SOFTWARE TIP:** We replaced the whiteboard system in the example above with a simple *'Resource Planner',* which was scalable, and just as easy to review. Check out http://www.patrena.com/ for the one we used, or why not check out *Google* to find a Cloud based equivalent.

## Lifestyle

Many businesses are lifestyle businesses, set up to support their owner's lifestyle and provide a certain level of income. Traditionally these businesses are not scalable and have limited growth because to attempt this would have a negative effect on the owner's lifestyle. These types of business can get away with not being too organised, but if you want your business to grow into more than this, then you do need the organisational elements we discuss in this book to be put into place.

Being organised cannot only affect your business, but also your life. If your business runs like clockwork and you get everything done within normal working hours, so when you go home you won't have to do the bookkeeping, update the website or answer emails – you can spend more time with your family or relaxing.

*An Organised Business = More Free Time*

If that's not the greatest reason for implementing tips I provide in this book, then I don't know what is?

We all know that when running a business, time or rather lack of it, can be your biggest enemy. It sometimes feels like there are never enough hours in the day to get everything done. Being organised will streamline everything and you will find that you have more time and less stress.

Some of the tips in later chapters will demand extra time from you, but the results will actually save you time in the long run.

## *What does being organised look like?*

- ✓ It's the opposite of looking frantic.
- ✓ It's being able to quickly and calmly access the information you need, and allows you to keep on top of all your deadlines.
- ✓ It's having a methodical approach to your work and being able to delegate in the confidence that it will get done.
- ✓ It's having the job run smoothly, whether it's a product that's delivered on time, or a service that's provided.
- ✓ It's where you've delighted your customer by pre-empting and overcoming any issues they may have had.
- ✓ It's being confident that the business can deliver excellence, without you being involved to make sure it does.

*The list goes on....*

### The 4 a.m. wake up call

Have you ever unexpectedly woken at 4 a.m. and been instantly wide-awake as all your worries, anxieties and 'to do's' come flooding into your head?

You lay there fretting about your business, worrying about how you are going to cope, how you are going to pay the bills or the taxman.

Isn't it ironic that your mind is waking you up at 4 a.m. to go through these things, but in reality this is the opposite of what you need to get things done the next day? You need more sleep, not less – but the worries overtake this need and you lay there wide-awake instead.

Having an *organised business* helps reduce the frequency of the 4 a.m. worrying sessions, because you know most aspects will be taken care of. In the organised business, things happen automatically. The 4 a.m. wake up calls may still happen, they are inevitable as a business owner, but it won't be worry about the business that keeps you awake – you'll find new things to fret about!

### The Tale of Two Brothers

*As mentioned earlier I'm now going to introduce the two business-owning brothers* **Stephen** *and* **John.**

**Stephen**, (the organised one) runs a business called '*Stephen Enterprises*'. It's a Turn-key Operation that doesn't rely on the owner running it; it operates smoothly and efficiently and gives Stephen very little stress and anxiety.

Needless to say, Stephen's business works, and when he goes on his three-week holidays, four times a year, it all runs smoothly without him. It's not necessarily driven in his absence, but the foundation of the business is solid. The orders come in, they get processed and delivered. There are systems in place for customer complaints, and there are feedback loops, which means that issues get resolved or escalated if there are any problems.

Growth is consistent and manageable. New staff can be hired because there are systems set in place for recruitment and training.

Stephen's business gives him the lifestyle he wants and has little impact on his home life. In fact, Stephen has just recently moved to a different county from where his business is located and only visits the premises two or three times a month. He now spends most of his time reviewing his *Key Performance Indicators* and working on his business. (*Key Performance Indicators*, or *KPIs*, are explained in more detail in *Chapter 7.*)

He makes it a rule to keep in contact with all his staff, and makes sure he goes back to the floor every now and again to experience the day-to-day running of his business.

Stephen's business is well organised, and well on the way to being a successful one.

**John** (the disorganised one) has a business that sells the same product and services as Stephens. In fact, they both started their businesses at the same time, but John's business only has half the sales. Why? Well, there are a few major differences between the two businesses. One is that John's sales and marketing department isn't organised, but the main one is because he doesn't think his business could cope with any more sales, and he actively discourages growth – he can't scale up because growth frightens him!

Even with less work to cope with, John's business is much more disorganised. There is no database, so customer details can't be found, and there are no proper systems for taking orders.

John gets embarrassed when products aren't delivered on time, or when the quality is sometimes questionable. He often gets exasperated with his staff and has even considered getting rid of them all, because he sometimes thinks that this will sort all of his worries out!

He can never take a holiday without things grinding to a halt. When he does take a break, he has to work twice as hard to make sure things are okay before he goes away, and then twice as hard when he gets back to get things back on track. The holiday seems pointless. In fact whilst on holiday, all John can think about is his business.

John's work doesn't stop when he gets home; his business is his life. It affects his marriage, because he's accused of always working. He can't switch off from his business – mainly because he can't afford to.

John never finds time to step back and work *on* the business; he's far too busy *in* it. In fact, the only time he works on it, is when he's on holiday – putting further pressure on his marriage.

The two businesses have *very different* effects on their owners' lives. They also have very different valuations; Stephen's business is *very sellable*, and worth **three times** as much as John's. John's business couldn't be sold, as there are no systems in place and no room for growth (hardly an inviting prospect for a future buyer).

So which business would you prefer to have? Stephen's or John's? I can probably guess which one!

## *An organised business will allow you;*

- ✓ To create a valuable, sellable business.
- ✓ To improve the quality of your customer experience.
- ✓ To improve your home life.
- ✓ To create more free time.

## Don't Be in Denial!

Many business owners are in denial about the state of their own businesses, and it's important that you occasionally take a step back from it and take an objective view of what your business really looks like. I will go into this in more detail in Chapter 3: Systemising, but it's worth taking a good look at your business to see if it operates how you had planned it when you started. Being in denial about where you are at is destructive and will not allow you to grow and be successful. This part will probably be the most difficult, but once you look at your business objectively, you might be surprised at how quickly you can turn things around.

If you have a disorganised business, and have never planned or undertaken a planning exercise, then this is where to start. In fact, this leads nicely on to the next chapter *'Organise Your Planning'.*

Even if you have done some planning in the past, then I still highly recommend you read the next chapter as you might learn some new ideas and strategies.

### To summarise:

An organised business is *much easier to run*, and will give you less stress and more free time in your life. The only way you can successfully grow and scale your business is by being organised; if you try to scale without doing this, then your chance of failure is high.

Taking an objective look at your business can also really help you understand where your business is at the moment, and help you see what you need to improve in it.

In this chapter I have introduced **Stephen** and **John**, so that you can see how two similar businesses can have major differences in results, and how being organised can be the difference between success and failure. Follow their story carefully and see how you can adopt and adapt some of the techniques that Stephen's business has to your own.

During the book we offer free resources that will, once implemented, help you along the way to becoming an organised business. These are available **for free for all readers of this book.** To access them visit **book.theorganisedbusiness.co.uk** and sign up for free membership.

# Chapter 2: Organise Your Planning

*"I love it when a plan comes together."*
**John 'Hannibal' Smith**

However your new business came about, when you first started you probably had a plan, either typed out, written down or in your head, but you most likely had a plan for exactly what you intended to do with your business.

 **Don't just read it, *do it!***

If you made a plan when you started out and you are able to find it, go and get it and have a good read.

➲ Tick off as many of the actions you feel you have achieved, and make a note of the ones you haven't.

I bet that you have achieved most of the things written down on the plan; that is if they were realistic targets. I would also bet that you haven't planned anything since that day.

If you haven't ever planned, then don't panic. Just make sure you do *all the exercises in this book*, and you will organically create a plan ready to springboard your business to the next level. This will also allow you to create a scalable business that is suitable to sell or pass on to a future generation, as and when you're ready.

## Planning is Essential

Planning is an *essential part of a successful business*, but the problem that most small businesses have, is that they are started by doers – action men and women who would much rather get on with it than plan it.

The entrepreneur, Richard Branson is famous for saying *"screw it, let's do it"*, but if you read his books, you will realise that he actually does *a lot* of planning and research *before* making any decisions.

You have probably all heard the famous adage, *'If you fail to plan you plan to fail'*, but maybe you haven't planned (or kept your planning up to date) because your time is taken up by the sheer volume of work you're doing.

If you can't cope at the moment, how are you going to make the time to plan?

### Real Life Example

I have many meetings with clients who are just starting out in business, but two in particular, that illustrate the need for planning, stick in my mind. Here are their stories;

#### An Italian Delicatessen

The first concerned a husband and wife who came to see me to talk about starting a new business. I asked a few questions, and discovered that the couple were going to invest £25,000 in an Italian Delicatessen in the town centre.

I asked if they had a plan, and if they had undertaken any market research for this project, and they answered *"no"* to both questions. I then asked if there was an Italian community in the town to serve, and they said that they didn't know.

I suggested they should at least do some market research, and find out the need for their service before committing their money. They didn't, and ended up investing well over £40,000. The business lasted less than a year, and they later told me that it was because it was situated in the wrong town. Sadly, it had failed due to a *lack of planning and research.*

## The Coach

The other conversation I had was with a coach. He came to me because the franchise he was buying required him to trade as a limited company.

We spoke about the coaching franchise in which he was about to invest £75,000. We discussed what research he had done (he had actually been quite thorough with it) but he hadn't spoken to many coaches outside of the ones provided by his particular franchise, and he didn't have any detailed plan in place.

In addition, he hadn't done any research into the customer base of the franchise to find out if they were likely to buy from him. I discouraged him from investing his life savings before doing some more investigation, and suggested he might be better off by investing £25,000 in some training and starting his own business.

However, he bought the franchise and to his credit, gave it 150%, trying to sell a product that no one wanted. He lasted six months before the business folded.

You may have noticed, that with both of these examples, I had asked about *their plan*, which *neither client had spent any time developing*.

These are two extreme examples, as most small businesses start up with very little capital, but ultimately it won't make any difference how much money you invest, if you haven't done your planning or research then your business will more than likely **fail**, so don't underestimate the importance of this stage.

Planning is *essential*, but it shouldn't be limited to the plan you make at the start of the business, *on-going planning* is even more vital, and I will go into how to do that later in the chapter.

Once you have made a plan, you will need to schedule a monthly review, to ensure that you are achieving what you have set out to do. I usually set aside one to two hours a month to do this. It's the first step in changing your disorganised business into an organised one, and investing this time will pay dividends later.

By regularly planning, and revisiting your plan you'll be steering your business towards your goal and vision.

> To use a nautical analogy, "It's far better, when steering a ship, to make frequent small course adjustments to keep towards the heading, than irregular large adjustments. The latter is time consuming, inefficient and could ultimately lead to you capsizing."

To stretch the ship analogy further, if as well as steering the ship, you are also trying to navigate, keep watch, serve the passengers and organise the crew, then it doesn't matter what you do, the ship will ultimately steer off-course as it's impossible to do all of the above effectively without an organised plan.

But more about that later, first let's catch up with our business owners Stephen and John.

## The Tale of Two Brothers

**John** had a plan when he began his business; he didn't write it down, but he knew what he needed to do. He didn't plan in minute detail, or set any time aside for putting pen to paper, but he did have a vision for what he wanted to achieve.

Problems arose when John needed to make key decisions for his business. He didn't have an overall plan to refer to, so instead of taking a direct route towards the business he wanted, he took an indirect route, with much trial and error.

These errors cost him time and money, and led to the business being disorganised, but it was the only way John knew. John is a man of action, not a man of planning.

These large course adjustments meant that something in the business had to be in crisis, or near it, before John took action – not because he didn't care, but because he had too many other tasks to do.

John has lost count of the number of times he nearly got to breaking point. Projects got started, but didn't get completed, they got lost on their way and usually had to be restarted. He had to hold crisis reorganisation days and spend days fire fighting problems over and over again.

These crises took up so much time, and caused so much stress and anxiety that it got to the point where John was permanently overloaded, which affected his life and health. Not a good situation to be in.

By contrast, as you would expect, **Stephen** did not fail to plan. In fact, he managed to strike the balance between enough planning and enough doing.

He understood that to build a successful business, it was essential to write down what he wanted his business to look like when it was finished, and Stephen did just that. He started out by summarising exactly what he wanted to achieve with his business, right at the beginning of the planning stage.

**The technique he used was to imagine what he wanted his business to look like in five years' time:**

- ✓ He wanted three vans and three teams delivering the service, and he wanted two sales people.

- ✓ He would run the business from home, but as soon as possible he would get an office. At first, the local serviced offices would be fine, but as he grew the business, he would get himself a unit.

- ✓ He knew that he would need an office-based team as well as one on the road, so he envisaged a manager and one assistant, along with himself.

- ✓ He thought about hiring a warehouse man, to manage the stock and keep the vans supplied, but that could wait for a year or two.

- ✓ He imagined his ideal customer, where they were based, and how he could keep them happy. He imagined his customers down to the last detail and researched them.

- ✓ He imagined what his website and his e-commerce site would look like, and what sort of experience it would give his customers.

*So even before he had an actual physical business, he had one on paper.*

He took this to the next level, and tried to understand what this new business would cost him. He created a spreadsheet with a timeline of five years, putting in costs against each element that he wanted. He built himself a cash flow based on what he wanted to achieve, and then used the costs to figure out what he needed to sell in order to make it happen. He didn't let the enormity of the vision dissuade him from his dream.

*As the saying goes, "How do you eat an elephant?*
*One bite at a time."*

Stephen's vision for the business was the elephant; he needed to break it down into small bite-sized portions, and that is exactly what he did. He reviewed his plan thus far, and produced a list of actions to undertake so that his grand vision was broken down into smaller and smaller chunks.

He could have stopped there, put the plan in a folder and forgot about it, but he didn't, he took the next step – and this is *crucial* - he set aside time, not only to action what he had listed, but also to *review* where he was against both the high level plan and the smaller achievable actions. At first he set aside two hours in his diary every week to review the plan, move it forward and adapt it. This then became something he could do once every two weeks and then once a month.

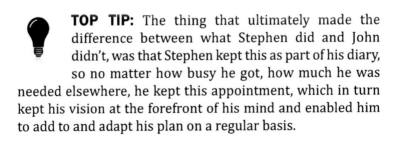

**TOP TIP:** The thing that ultimately made the difference between what Stephen did and John didn't, was that Stephen kept this as part of his diary, so no matter how busy he got, how much he was needed elsewhere, he kept this appointment, which in turn kept his vision at the forefront of his mind and enabled him to add to and adapt his plan on a regular basis.

## Writing a vision for your business

If you have never written a vision for your business, then these next steps are for you. If you have written one, then go and get it and check it meets all of the following criteria:

### Step 1

**Writing your vision for your business.** There is a simple technique for doing this, and that is to imagine what your business will be like at some point in the future, let's say five years.

What do you want your business to become, and what do you want your role in it to be?

Imagine it's 8 a.m. on a sunny day, and you're driving to work. You arrive at your office, park the car and walk through the doors past the factory, past the warehouse, what do you see?

- ➲ How many people are there?
- ➲ What are your offices like?
- ➲ Who are your customers?
- ➲ What are your products or service?
- ➲ What is your role in the business?
- ➲ How much time are you working in it?
- ➲ How much do you earn from the business?
- ➲ How much time do you set aside to work in the business?
- ➲ Describe how the business runs? Is it efficient, organised etc.?

Answer these questions, and any more you can think of, in as much detail as you can and you will have a good idea of what the business will look like in five years' time.

Now summarise the above into a neat paragraph or two, with a heading such as *"What my business will become,"* or *"Where I want to take my business,"* or *"xxxxx Ltd. in the year xxxx".*

## Step 2

Accurately describe your business as it is at present, using all the above questions you used to describe your business in the future.

Again, summarise the present reality into a couple of paragraphs, titled *"What my business is now".*

## Step 3

Compare the two descriptions and consider the key differences between the business you have now and the business you will have in the future.

## Step 4

**With all this in mind write up your vision**. Try to keep it as short as possible, but long enough that is sums up what you want your business to become in as much detail as necessary to make a third party understand.

This process above should give you a vision that contains all these elements if not more:

- A vision for the future.
- Things that will work well.
- The customer experience.
- Your role in the future business.
- Your salary expectations.
- Your exit strategy.
- Your business core values.

- Key performance targets for the next five years.

  *Achieving the vision:*

- Problems to resolve.

- Other items that need work in order to achieve the vision.

- Issues to resolve in core values.

- Areas to improve the customer experience.

- Additional action to take to achieve performance targets.

Once you have *all this written down* and your vision in place, you will be amazed at how quickly things will start to get focused, you will immediately be ahead of the game and planning will become much easier.

### Don't just read it, *do it!*

Now is the time to write down your vision. You don't have to nail it first time, but if you don't already have one, then you need a vision for your business and now is the time to do it. Follow the steps outlined above and complete this step. Remember, actions speak louder than words so *don't skip this stage.*

---

If you haven't already, why not take a visit to; **book.theorganisedbusiness.co.uk** and download *'The Organised Business Workbook'* that accompanies this book, as it will help you achieve the things I've asked you to do. Go and download it now!

# Plan of Action

*"In the long run, men hit only what they aim at."*
**Henry David Thoreau**

I believe the *simple act* of writing down plans can actually make them happen, as long you are positive, you can achieve the goals you are working towards.

So now you have a vision of what your business will become, we need to break this down into more manageable chunks, so we can set about achieving it.

## *The 'Action Plan'*

The next step is to review the information you've gathered, and come up with a list of *actions* that need to be completed in order to get your vision implemented. These will be split between short, medium and long-term actions.

As I mentioned in the introduction, I highly recommend you keep notes as you go through book, ideally in *'The Organised Business Workbook'*. In later chapters I suggest ideas and techniques for you to implement along the way; so it's really important to do them in order to keep on track with your vision of your business.

### What has to change to make the vision a reality?

Some of these actions will be easy to implement, and some will be harder. If you feel that an action point is too difficult, introduce another action before that one to make it easier. For example, if your action point is to *attract new customers*, then consider reviewing how you are going to do this, e.g. increase marketing. Next, take this a step further and write down your *'Marketing Plan'* (Chapter 5 has some great ideas for that).

I have found that it is best to work backwards from your vision, and start with some high level actions, your immediate vision goals. These are the final things you would need to action in order to achieve your vision.

Then try to break these immediate vision goals down into smaller goals, or second tier vision goals. If need be go to a third tier.

**Let me give you an example:**

In your vision, you may have imagined a Manager running things, so your *immediate vision goal is;*

- **Take on a manager.**

To achieve this, you would need to; (*second tier vision goals*)

- Outline their role.
- Figure out what tasks they will be doing.
- Achieve £10,000 a month in sales to pay for them.
- Get an office, so they have a place to work from.

You may need to break these down into even smaller chunks. Continue until you have a clear route from where you are now, right up to your top tier vision.

**SOFTWARE TIP:** A good tool for this is mind-mapping software, such as *www.mindmeister.com* or *www.mindgenius.com* these allow you to map out a central theme and then break this down into smaller chunks.

At the end of this process, you should have;

- ✓ a vision,
- ✓ some high level goals (immediate vision goals) and
- ✓ some smaller goals (second tier goals).

This should give you the road map from where you are now, through to where you want to be.

Don't worry too much if your action plan is a bit messy, as long as each action brings you a step closer to your final vision.

## Using the vision

As well as helping you define individual actions, your vision can also help you make decisions in the business – here's how.

Whenever you make a decision that is strategic in nature, and that will have an effect on the direction of the business, you should be asking yourself, *"Does this meet with the vision I have for this business? Does this decision help move me towards or away from the vision that I had for the business?"* This way the vision is at the forefront of your mind during these crucial times.

Once complete, I suggest printing your vision onto a piece of paper, laminating it and placing it prominently so that all your new employees can see it. You will be amazed how well a vision can galvanise both employees and managers.

### To summarise:

Planning is an *essential part* of any successful business, and failure to create one, and to keep it updated could cause your business to fail – or at least stop it from being scalable and sellable.

To successfully plan you need to do the following:

- Record your progress in *'The Organised Business Workbook".*

- Create a vision (using the steps outlined on page 32) by imagining what your business looks like now, and what it will look like in five years' time, and ultimately when it's ready to sell.

- Use the ideas above to produce an action plan, to take you from where the business is now to where your vision could take it.

- Break these actions down into smaller and smaller actions and set time aside each week to review them.

- Make sure everyone, including you, knows what your vision is.

- *Do the exercises!*

- Set time aside each month to review the plan and measure how you are doing against it.

- When making key strategic decisions ask yourself, *"Does this fit in with the plan"?*

# Chapter 3: Organise Your Systems

*"If you can't describe what you are doing as a process, you don't know what you're doing."*
**W. Edwards Deming, Total Quality Management**

## PART 1: Systemise Your Business

By systemise, I mean to *create processes and procedures* made up of flow charts, instructions, forms, checklists and templates to facilitate the smooth running of your business.

These systems allow you to be confident that the work which needs to be done in your business will be completed in the same way every time, by whoever is tasked to undertake it.

Systemising (the processes of creating these internal systems) is ultimately about creating a business that does not rely on *you*, or the skill of any individual, but rather on *the system* and the person's ability to follow it.

Every business, and I really do mean *every* business, can and should use systems to a more or lesser extent. All successful medium-to large businesses have documented systems in place.

### Systems thinking

To think in a systemised way in this context, is to look at your business or elements in your business, with a detached viewpoint so that you can concentrate on developing the business by working **on** *it*, not *in it*.

The aim of this is to give you an impartial view as to what's going on, although this is often very difficult to do. In fact, with many of my clients, I ask them to physically remove themselves from their business so we can focus; otherwise there are just too many distractions.

The reaction, when I ask them to do this often makes me chuckle, as it's nearly always the same. A look of horror at the thought of taking a day off from the business, followed by the resignation that it needs to be done.

This impartial view of what is going wrong in the business is essential if you are going to try and fix it. This is why business coaching and mentoring works, because coaches have an impartial view. I want you to try and take an impartial view of your own business and develop your own systems. No one knows your business better than you so you are in the ideal position to put things into place.

## Roles

*Often, small business owners find it difficult to separate the roles that they play in their own businesses.*

This is because when they are busy working *in* the business, getting involved with elements that they know they really shouldn't be doing, and barely coping with the pressures and strains this entails, outlining these roles doesn't come at the top of their list. However, this is steeped in irony, because the only way to stop doing the things they shouldn't be doing and to relieve the pressure they are under, is to learn to separate them with the ultimate aim of delegating the elements that then can be done by someone else.

The role of **owner/shareholder** is actually a passive one and they should not be actively involved in the day-to-day running of the business at all. Imagine you own shares in a big company like British Airways, for example. Apart from attending a few meetings a year where you vote on the directors' remuneration package, there is nothing much else involved.

The role of **MD/CEO** is one of leader, motivator and decision maker. The shareholders might be consulted, but this will be rare. This role controls the strategic and operational decisions for the business.

When the owner/manager is doing the work that the business does, he then becomes a **technician**. This role is not to make decisions, to own, or to do anything else other than be an employee of the business, and when the employees start making decisions, that's when things can begin to go wrong.

## The mix

In a small business, especially in the early years, one person may have to do a *mix of roles*, and there is nothing wrong with this, but ultimately, the aim for your business is to separate these roles out. The biggest battle is to recognise the roles you are actively involved in and acknowledge that they can be split up (for example, Owner, MD and employee) and then *delegated* accordingly.

This chapter explains why this is so important and why you need to be thinking along these lines. It explains what many of the world's largest businesses do, and what you need to know about using systems to organise your business.

## *Why you should systemise*

The majority of small businesses are over-reliant on their owners. It's probably true in your business, and it's probably true of everyone you know in business.

The reason is that most small business owners start a business to do something; to either produce something, to provide a service, or deliver a product. Very few businesses are started by people who want to *run* a business, and it's critical you understand the difference.

In fact, what often happens is that the person starting the business was probably originally an employee of another business, and one day they had a light bulb moment when they knew that they could do that type of work better if they started on their own.

> ### Warning!
>
> If you employ someone who has once run their own business for any length of time and they have lost it (for whatever reason), unless you are giving them a lot of freedom, which goes against the systems approach, you are making a big mistake. The reason is that they will find it difficult to work for anyone else, and you may not get the best out of them because they will want to do it their way and not your way. *There are exceptions but beware.*

So the doing of the work gets confused with the running of the business. It's inevitable, because in the early years you were probably doing just that... all the doing!

However, as the business grows this will need to change, and unless you can transform yourself from the person providing the service into the business owner, then your business will suffer.

Of course, this reliance on the owner is absolutely necessary in the early stages of a business, as it requires building up. There probably won't be enough resources (or money) for this not to be the case. You can't just throw new people at the business with limited funds, so you probably will need to do everything.

However this nurturing relationship that exists at the beginning of the business will, in the long run, stifle, restrict and destroy the business's chance of becoming a medium or large operation, because you won't be able to grow. You can only do so much on your own!

---

### Real Life Example

Every day I see examples of over-reliance, with the business owner, working *in* the business, not *on* it.

**One such example is a business owner called Harry:**

Harry sells fantastic high-end kitchens. Electric drawers, boiling water taps, inductive hobs, you name it, his kitchens do it. He's very successful, with orders coming out of his ears, but he isn't happy; he's stressed because he is the business.

He spends all day and night working *in* the business, keeping track of quotes, organising visits, even fitting the kitchens himself.

His friends say that's all he does. They also say he is really disorganised. This isn't true though, he has some organisational skills, but what he lacks is a *systemised approach* to organisation, and this results in his business not being scalable.

Harry takes on staff, but he sets himself up for problems because he doesn't define the roles and tasks that these staff should do before they start.

Harry is an ideal client for these planning strategies, and we are working together to free him from the business, and set it up so it can be taken to the next level.

---

If you own a small business which is controlled and closely run by yourself, and you're happy not to grow it and maximise the potential it has, then that's fine. But if you want a business that can be grown, and ultimately sold, then you need to adapt your role and the systems that exist within it.

Small businesses are the backbone of the economy; my father ran such a business, but I know he wanted more for it. He wanted it to grow, to leave a legacy to us, his children, but in truth he didn't know how to do it. He was smart enough, fantastic with people, had more than his fair share of the get up and go needed, but he couldn't make it happen because he didn't have the tools to achieve it.

That is where this book will help you, as long as you action the points and strategies outlined. If you want a larger more successful business, then you must change your relationship with the business, and one way to do this is to systemise.

Change the way you view your role in the business and aim to work on it.

### The Tale of Two Brothers

**John** *didn't systemise;* he didn't realise that he was working too much *in* the business, and he never worked *on* the business unless something was in crisis.

He continued his approach of making large course adjustments when there was a major issue, and applied this to improving the business. If nothing went wrong, then he didn't fix it. In fact, he kept his head down and hoped it would all work out.

The major problems occurred when John took on staff. He failed to define their roles and responsibilities, which meant tasks that they should have been doing, were not clearly defined. Inevitably, those tasks tended to be done how the staff member wanted to do them – in short; they did it their way.

Again, this was fine when the business was small with one or two members of staff. John could spot errors, and react to make sure things were right. It caused frustration, but it worked for the most part. But as the business grew, John got increasingly frustrated with the amount of things that went wrong, and he blamed it on not being able to get good people. He couldn't see that it wasn't the people but the system (or lack of) that was causing the problems.

People are resourceful, and the lack of a defined system will cause them to try and find the best way of doing things. The problems occurred because John's employees were making these decisions, but they lacked John's knowledge and understanding of the business, so ultimately these decisions were wrong, and they cost the business money.

Another issue was with processes. These were not clearly mapped out and explained, so the delivery of the product or service was not uniform, which led to the customer experience not always being consistent. Sometimes the customer was asked for their feedback, sometimes not, sometimes the product was on time, and sometimes it wasn't.

Finally, there were no checklists in place, no one was sure if everything was being completed on each job, so inevitably some things weren't completed correctly, if at all.

John thought he had a bunch of Muppets working for him, and he thought about getting rid of the lot of them. The only time things went well in the business was when John did it himself.

**Stephen**, on the other hand, had systemised his business. His vision stated that in five years' time, he would have a fully systemised business. He had read the books and understood the concepts, and early on he defined the roles that not only existed in his business now, but in his business of the future. He understood that these roles, whilst he was doing them at the moment, would not be his forever, so he set about recording exactly how he wanted them done, so that when it came to delegate them, they could be easily followed. Stephen mapped out the processes in the business, starting with the sales process, and recorded each step so he could see that his business worked. Systems were everywhere.

In contrast to John, Stephen set time to work *on* the business and tried to avoid the mistake of working too much *in* it.

Every time he took on an employee he followed the recruitment process, which meant all employees were recruited in the same way. They knew what was expected from them, and what behaviour was acceptable and unacceptable from day one. Their induction process introduced them to the concept of systems. They were shown the sales process and the importance of systems within that.

The systems in Stephen's business ensured that when Stephen took on people, he could be more confident that the work would continue in the way he wanted it done and that this process gradually freed him from the business.

This took a while, but the process started the moment he could delegate some work, confident in the knowledge that it would be done correctly, so he could focus on working more *on* the business.

Of course there were setbacks along the way. The culture of following these systems had to be ingrained into all new staff, and a few couldn't or wouldn't buy into that, so they had to go.

When it came to selling the business, Stephen's system culture and physical systems greatly increased the value to a potential purchaser, because they wouldn't have to do anything other than learn and tweak the systems already set in place.

On the other hand, John's business still needed a lot of work to make it efficient and not reliant on him, the owner, and this then reflected in the sale price.

## How to systemise your business

Systemising is the process of identifying all the roles, tasks, forms and checklists that exist in the business, not just yours or your employees, but all possible roles that currently exist or could exist in the future.

Systemising is a journey that once started, will never be finished, but along the way you will see massive improvements to your business, employees and life. Are you ready to begin?

**A Warning before you go on** – this chapter is heavy going, with some quite intense exercises. It would be worth reading through it once and then coming back to it and trying each stage of the process of systemising again. To fully systemise can take years; so don't rush through the exercises I outline here.

There are a few exercises you need to do to get started, and whilst you might not immediately see the benefit, roll with it, things will come together.

*We start our journey by identifying the roles that exist in your business:*

## The roles

To start with, you have to start thinking of your people as roles, because in systems thinking, these people are fulfilling roles in the business, and you need to think of them in that way.

If you don't employ anyone yet, imagine that your business is much larger than it is. You still have roles; only you are doing them all.

These roles generally fall into two types; **individual roles** and **shared roles.**

An **individual role** is a role where it is necessary that only one person is deployed to do it. These roles are important because the responsibility rests with one person.

*Examples of individual roles are:*

- Managing Director.
- Operations Manager.
- General Manger.
- Contracts Manager.
- IT Manager.

These are *key roles*, managing and co-ordinating operations. Only one person should be responsible for each of these roles. (Unfortunately, in most small businesses the owner is responsible for more than one of these.)

The individual role doesn't have to be a manager, although it generally is. Anything you can think of that needs to be done by just one person, however big your business gets, is an individual role.

The other type of role is a **shared role**, which several people can undertake.

A **shared role** is not inferior to an individual role; some of the most important roles are shared roles.

*Examples of shared roles are:*

- Salesperson.

- Bookkeeper.

- Receptionist.

- Fitter.

- Designer.

- Surveyor.

These are roles where more than one person shares a position. The role they do is the same whether they do it for a particular area, or in a particular department.

There may only be one person doing the shared role at this moment, but it doesn't make it an individual role, it's still a shared role, you just haven't needed to hire the extra staff yet.

### Don't just read it, *do it!*

Identifying the roles – shared and individual – is the first step you are about to take to make your business scalable. On a piece of A4 paper, write the heading of *'Roles in my Business'.* Draw a line down the centre and title the two sub columns '**Shared**' and '**Individual Roles**' (if you're using the workbook, this has already been done for you.)

- ⮑ Now write down all the roles you can think of in your business, placing them under the correct headings.

- ⮑ If you have trouble categorising the roles under these headings, then it might help for you to imagine your business as being much larger. A larger business will have more than one person doing a specific role.

&#10162; You may find all your roles are shared roles –
that's fine, except for Managing Director, which should
be an individual role.

&#10162; Next underneath each role, write the name of the
person or persons currently doing them in your
business.

*After you have done the exercise above you will recognise
several things:*

- You're probably taking on too many roles!

- Some roles should be individual and are currently
being shared. This is when mistakes happen and
things get missed.

- There are far more roles than you realised.

You can make immediate systems improvements by
correcting some of these things now, but don't do too much as
there are other things you need to consider.

## Processes

> *"Apple is a very disciplined company, and we have great
> processes... Process makes you more efficient."*
> **Steve Jobs**

Processes are the heart of any business, and process mapping
is a very valuable exercise.

Process mapping can be over-complicated and jargon-filled,
so I will explain what it is and how to do it as simply as
possible.

Process mapping, in the context of this book, is simply writing
out the steps in any process, identifying the beginning and
then writing down each step to see what happens next.

This can be done on a piece of paper, using a software program or with sticky notes on a wall.

The act of mapping out these processes will highlight inefficiencies in the business.

## Types of processes

There are *two types* of processes we can map, **multi-role** processes, and **single-role** processes.

**Single-role** processes are, as the name suggests, processes that are contained in one role, and only one role needs to be involved in that process from the beginning to the end.

*Some examples of a single role process are:*

- **Opening the post.**
- **Ordering Stationary.**
- **Credit Control.**

That is not to say you might have enough work for two credit controllers, but they are both doing the shared role of credit controller, and that role contains one single role process of credit control. That is to say the process does not require the interaction of the other roles for it to be completed. The credit controller can do the role from beginning to end on their own in isolation.

**Multi-role** processes. These are processes that require the interaction of several roles to complete the process.

Several roles need to collaborate and work together to get the job done. The best example, as we will see in more detail later, is the sales process.

It is important to understand the difference because, as you will see, multi-role processes are more difficult to map out and think about as they require the interaction of different roles, and ultimately people.

## Mapping single-role processes

These are the simplest to map and cause the least problems in the business. An example of a single-role process is doing any regular task. The regular stationary order is a good example. You monitor it, and when it runs low, you order more. No interaction between roles is necessary.

The best way to map single-role process is to ask the person who is doing the role to write down the steps they take when doing the process.

*For example, ordering the stationery would be:*

- Check stationary cupboard for stationery levels.
- Identify what needs ordering.
- Make a list.
- Phone supplier A with list.
- Await order.
- When order arrives check against list.
- Put stationery in cupboard.

You may be thinking, why bother documenting single-role processes? Well, there are really two reasons for doing this:

1. It is a good introduction to process mapping – it starts you thinking through how a process fits together.

2. A lot can go wrong in a simple process that you have no control over. Before I mapped the stationary order, I just thought it magically appeared. I didn't realise we were using supplier A, to be honest I didn't have time to worry, but I now know supplier A is the most expensive supplier; I would prefer to use supplier B and save money.

By mapping even these simple processes and reviewing how these are done, efficiency can be improved and money saved, plus this procedure will be done exactly the same way every time, and anyone who can follow instructions can do it.

### Don't just read it, *do it!*

In your workbook, make a list of all the **single-role** processes that exist in your business; remember single-role processes are ones where one role will complete the task. If it helps, think of this as one person completing the task.

➲ Identify as many as possible.

➲ To get used to mapping them pick the key ones, you will want to do them all eventually, but start with one thing at a time.

## Mapping multi-role processes

These are harder to map because they involve the interaction between roles in your business. What's more, whilst you are mapping you will be trying to improve the process as you go.

It may be easier to think of mapping multi-role processes as a 3D jigsaw that you are going to put together. The best place to start is to make a list of all the multi-role processes you can think of that exist in your business.

Here are some examples of multi-role processes, the processes in your business will probably differ from these but they should give you the idea of the mapping process.

*Examples of multi-role processes are:*

- **The sales process**
- **Recruitment**
- **Stock control**
- **Deliveries**
- **Bookkeeping**
- **Marketing**
- **Purchasing**

*Next identify the sub processes that may exist under these headings:*

**The sales process**

- Initial enquiry
- Follow up
- Sales meeting
- Taking the order
- Processing the order
- Despatch of goods
- Invoicing
- Dealing with complaints

**Recruitment**

- Deciding on method of advertising
- Short listing
- The interview
- Before the individual starts
- Induction

**Stock Control**

- Taking deliveries
- Keeping stock level up to date
- Removing stock
- Ordering stock
- Stock taking

**Deliveries**

- Receiving the delivery
- Checking it against the purchase orders
- What to do if the delivery is incorrect
- Next steps if the delivery is correct

**Bookkeeping:**

- Invoicing
- Paying suppliers
- Receiving money
- VAT
- Month-end routine
- Running wages

**Marketing**

- Deciding on campaigns
- Designing material
- Despatch of material
- Follow-up

**Purchasing**

- Deciding on supplier list
- Deciding on item to be purchased
- Seeking approval
- Ordering
- Taking delivery
- Receipt of invoices

You can see that each of these **multi-role** processes is now broken down into sub-processes. Some of these processes may be able to be broken down further, and some will be at their lowest part.

If processes can be broken down further, do so until you have the lowest component.

### Don't just read it, *do it!*

In your workbook make a list of all the multi- role processes that exist in your business: Remember multi-role processes are ones where more than one role will complete the task. If it helps, think of this as more than one person completing the task.

⊃ Identify as many as possible.

⊃ Identify the sub-processes that exist.

## For the visualists among you:

If you tend to think more visually, then a good exercise at this point is to prepare flow charts for the processes you have identified. For the purposes of this initial flow chart we will use the multi-role processes you have identified and then map out a process using the first sub-processes.

As an example, the sales process (a multi role-process) for my accountancy practice is here:

### Accsys Accountants Ltd

## SALES PROCESS - Flowchart

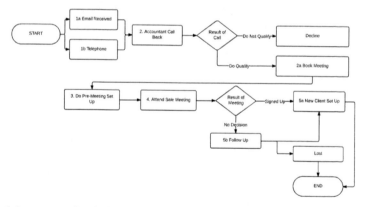

*(please go to book.theorganisedbusiness.co.uk for a full PDF printout)*

 **SOFTWARE TIP:** I often use www.lucidchart.com/ for my flow charts - It's free for up to 60 components in any one flowchart, and easy to use. It has a great feature for identifying when a process flips between roles called Swim lanes. These simple lines when added to a process allow you to easily identify when a process changes role.

## The sales process

When I'm process mapping, I always start with the sales process, as it will have the biggest impact in your business if there is something wrong. Start with the initial enquiry, and work right through until you have delivered the product or service and been paid. Don't forget to ask for customer feedback as the last thing you do.

## The devil is in the detail

The sales process outlined next is for example only; your sales process will be tailored to your company

Earlier we started by identifying sub-processes that could be included under multi-role processes and for the sales process we came up with this:

- Initial enquiry
- The follow-up
- The sales meeting
- Taking the order
- Processing order
- Despatch of goods
- Invoicing
- Dealing with complaints

Next we will flesh out some details. This doesn't have to be perfect yet; we're still just brainstorming on the process (always try and brainstorm with someone else, *it really helps*).

Ultimately, you are looking to create a step-by-step instruction list of how you want each step to be done. This won't be completed in the first sitting; it will be re-visited again and again, until you have covered everything, but you have to start somewhere, so here goes.

At first, we are going to make some high level notes, of how you want this process done.

**For example:**

*Initial enquiry*

This could be received via email or telephone. If the initial enquiry is received by email, you will need to call the customer back, when you make this call it's important that you know what goals you are aiming for. These are:

1. To make a good impression; this might be the first contact with the customer.

2. To find out what the customer wants from you.

3. To qualify the customer.

4. To find out where the customer heard about you.

5. If they qualify to book a sales meeting.

If you answer the call, as opposed to calling them back, then always answer the phone in the following way:

*"Good morning, company name, John speaking"*

During the call, answer the customer queries, but always be steering the conversation towards the aims of the call.

*How to qualify the customer*

Whilst on the call be aware of what makes a good customer for our business. We are looking for things such as, do they have the budget, are they located in the area we want to sell in, do we want to work with this customer?

*At the end of the call*

Either put the call through to a surveyor/salesperson, book a meeting for the surveyor/salesperson in their diary or if they're not available enter the message into a 'Calls to follow up' list on the database and set a reminder for the surveyor / salesperson to follow this up.

### The follow up

The surveyor/salesperson then follows up the call and ascertains exactly what is required. The aim of this call is to either book an appointment to visit the company, or a sale.

If it is an appointment, then it is put into the *'appointments diary'.*

### The sales meeting

Check the *'appointments diary'* to ascertain when the appointment is.

Hopefully you can see how this is going. We are outlining each step of the sub-process in as much detail as we can. Unfortunately, there are no shortcuts, believe me I have tried.

Once you have written out all your notes for the entire sales process, you will probably have a jumbled set of instructions of how you believe the sales process works.

In the end this will have to be completed for each process that we have identified. This will create an operations manual for your business.

**Here are some tools that can be used to help record this list:**

- ✓ A digital Dictaphone is great for recording your thoughts. This can then be given to someone to type up, or alternatively Google *'Digital transcription.'* to find a third party to do this.

- ✓ Sticky notes often help mapping by laying out a process in blocks on any surface.

- ✓ Visit http://www.mindmeister.com/ or download an app. for mind mapping software, perfect for the early stages of the process.

- ✓ I often use https://www.lucidchart.com/ for my flow charts - It's free for up to 60 components in any one flowchart, easy to use as well.

✓  Google Chrome has a number of flowcharting add-ons.

✓  The best tool at this stage by far, is a blank piece of paper, a quiet room, and someone who knows how the process works or should work (probably you).

So by now, you should have your processes identified, your sub-processes identified and some details added, (don't worry if this a bit jumbled at the moment). You also have your list of roles, and it's now time to join the two together. For each step of the process allocate a role to that step.

I'll continue using the sales process as an example:

| Sales process steps | Roles that could do these steps |
|---|---|
| Initial enquiry | Telephone receptionist |
| The follow-up | The salesperson |
| The sales meeting | The salesperson |
| Taking the order | The salesperson |
| Processing the order | Sales assistant |
| Despatch of goods | Warehouse person |
| Invoicing | Bookkeeper |
| Dealing with complaints | Customer Service Manager |

Now you have the roles allocated, it's time to refine your previous ramblings into how each step of the process should look.

Put the notes you made into an easy-to-follow instruction list. Whilst doing this, rethink the detail and whether this is the best way to do this process (now is a good time to make improvements to the process). You can give it to another member of your team, and ask them to follow your instructions to the letter – you'll soon see if there is anything missing!

This process is *time consuming*, but I estimate you will save ten times the amount of time you put in over the short to medium term, and hundreds of times over the long run.

Described above is a generic sales process but to give you a further example, *here is what a completed process looks like in my accountancy business*. You have already seen the flow chart for this earlier in the chapter.

---

### Real Life Example

**In my business**

Here is an example of a brainstormed sales process for my accountancy business. This is the direct result of brainstorming the process and the roles that exist.

At this stage, we weren't finished. We went on to explain exactly how things were to be done, but this gives you an idea of what you want to achieve for each process.

#### 1. Sales Enquiry

*1.1. Email Contact*

Scan email for all relevant details – is contact looking for an accountant's service? Complete the top of telephone enquiry form (this form will be used in stage 2 – the accountant's call).

Call to find out any missing information if the number has

---

been provided, if not email and obtain the contact number.

*1.2. Telephone Contact*

Answer phone – Good morning/afternoon Accsys  xxxx speaking.

Complete the top of the telephone enquiry form with as much information as possible.

Explain that we will get an accountant to call them back.

Pass the form to an accountant.

Add new client to New Enquiry on Workflow Max* (explained below).

## *2. Accountant's Call*

2.1 If calling back, research business. Five-minute research – Credit Check/Website/Enquiry Form.

2.2 Call client. During call, complete the rest of the form and book a meeting if the client qualifies.

Using Google Diary, set up a reminder to call the day before the meeting to confirm.

Enter details of the meeting on form.

2.2.A   After the call (if the client qualifies).

Set up the job on Workflowmax. Add client to potential group and set up a potential client job.

Hand back the enquiry form to assistant.

2.2.B   After call (If the client does not qualify).

Complete standard referral email and send to referral partners.

Change group to referral given.

### *3. Pre-client Meeting Set Up*

3.1 Put Meeting Pack together – It should contain the following:

- Engagement letter.
- 64-8.
- Service summary.
- Business card.
- Companies House information – Webcheck – if Ltd Company.
- Credit Check Information – Summary Report – if Ltd Company.
- Price List – Make sure it is current and up-to-date.
- Label on pack with name and date of meeting on it.
- Sales enquiry form.
- Sales meeting form – Refer to telephone enquiry form for guidance on which form (NB, EB, GB).

3.2 Tick off pre-set up checklists on job on workflow.

3.3 Place pack into accountant's new client meeting tray.

### *4. New Client Meeting (Accountant)*

4.1 Make sure you know the time and place of the meeting and whom it is with.

4.2 First half of the meeting;

Ask questions following the format of the form. Do not limit your questions to just to the ones on the form – go with it.

4.3 Second half of meeting;

- Explain service summary, why we do not record time, why we started the firm and have each level of service.

- Ensure you are relating the services to their individual needs, to demonstrate that they are getting a tailored service.

- Calculate and explain the price.

- Explain the engagement letter, wait and complete form with them.

- If they sign the engagement letter, explain what happens next.

- Fill out the 64-8 Form and get them to sign it.

- Pass back to assistant.

5.1. If Client signs up

### *Assistant's jobs*

- Find potential client on Workflow and change to relevant service group and to existing or current client.

- Set up new client job.

- Give client reference number, first letter of business name plus next number available – refer to existing client ref list.

- Set up folders:

  - Paper folder – blue folder, with a permanent marker write on client name and reference number.

  - Electronic Folder – In *'Doc Store.'*

- Prepare 12 month invoice using the template in Microsoft Word and save in electronic folder.

- Prepare Gocardless pay link.

- Prepare as much of the welcome email that you are able to and save a copy into the electronic folder in outlook message format.

- Pass paper folder to accountant.

- Prepare clearance letter.

### *Accountant's Jobs*

- Review and update workflow checklist to remove unnecessary items.

- Finish invoice.

- Review and complete welcome email.

- Set up on finance pack.

- Review and send clearance letter.

5.2. If client does not sign up straight away

- Assistant to enter in diary first follow up phone call seven days after the initial meeting – for accountant.

- After call, do one of the following:
    - Move to lost jobs.
    - Book another phone call for seven days time and  repeat until either lost or they sign up.

- Client signs up if so refer to 5.1.

5.3. Lost.

Move to lost on Workflow. Put paper in lost client in filing cabinet.

**TOP TIP:** In this example I mentioned a few tools and programs that we use, to help organise our business. These items include:

- *Telephone enquiry form* – it is worth having these if you want to qualify the contact or have set questions you want to ask with each call. Another option is to have the form on your CRM – Customer Relationship Database

- *Workflow Max* – This is a cloud based CRM and workflow system (other software is available). Workflow works on checklists that are set up and allocated to different members of staff. This means that when a job comes in, it is allocated to a salesperson and added to their 'to do' list. They then have a checklist to follow for this task. This can mean that the whole process can be smooth and efficient. Check it out at *www.workflowmax.com.*

- *Sales team diary* – A central diary for organising your business is a great idea. An affordable way to achieve this is with Google Calendar, another option is to set it up in Outlook. Either way it should be easily accessible by all staff members.

- *Sales meeting form* – A form to take to your sales meeting is an invaluable tool. It makes sure you ask all the questions and gather all the correct information. Plus if you make notes during your sales meeting, it shows that you are interested and want to retain the information gathered.  See *Chapter 5 – Organise Your Sales and Marketing.*

### The links

Now you have the roles and a process that flows through the roles defined, let's think about how these roles *link together*. The best way to describe this is to imagine it's only you in the business, and you do everything from initial enquiry to despatch.

If you are doing each of these roles, then the links are easy as you are doing them all.

Now take on a salesperson and a goods dispatcher. How do you tell your salesperson that they have a meeting booked, and how does the salesperson tell the dispatcher that a product has to go out? Maybe just by communicating with each other?

However, imagine you have a team of salespeople, a telephone reception team, and a team of dispatchers. Now you will have to have more sophisticated methods.

Imagine the processes flowing through a different person at each step. Of course, this may not be the case at the moment in your business, but we are thinking big.

**So how does one process link to another?** *The links occur at the moment the process passes between roles.*

For example, the receptionist takes the initial enquiry and determines that a follow-up call will be required. The receptionist must somehow tell the salesperson, and to do this, I would suggest a standard email to the sales team, plus an update to the '*sales team diary*'. This is the *link* between the roles in a multi-role process.

The sales team, upon receipt of the email, will call with the aim of arranging a meeting, and a standard 'sales meeting form' is completed whilst on the phone, with all the details required.

In this case this is saved to a central file storage called the '*Document Store*' under '*Potential Customers*' in the following file format; **Name: YYYY.MMM.DD Sales Meeting Form.doc.** *(In Chapter 4: The organised Computer,* we go into why a **central file storage facility** is important for the organised business and why saving your documents in the above format will make it much easier to find documents.)

A meeting is placed in the diary, and the salesperson that will attend is notified by email.

*This is another link in the multi-role sales process.*

The *meeting step* starts when the salesperson receives the email and prints the meeting form. The meeting step ends after the meeting, with either a sale being made, or not. If a sale is made, the order should be taken by the salesperson.

The next step is *processing the order*, which requires a switch in the role doing the task.

The salesperson emails the sales assistant with the order attached, and they take relevant details to complete the order form in duplicate. One copy goes to the bookkeeper; one goes to the dispatcher.

The bookkeeper will then raise an invoice and pass it to the dispatcher who will, when he receives both invoice and order, complete the order and dispatch it.

This is a simplified process, and there may be other steps to take, for example, if something happens other than an order, or if an item is not in stock to be dispatched.

I hope you can now see how to start mapping the processes, and that only by doing this can efficiencies be weaned from each and every processes.

You may be thinking that this is going to take a long time, and you would be correct. This will take a considerable amount of investment in your business, *but* the time savings will become apparent with every process you complete. This becomes a snowball effect, and pretty soon you will be flying.

*So let's review what we have covered so far, and hopefully what you now have identified (or will be working towards):*

- ⮩ You have the roles that exist in your business, which have been split into individual roles and shared roles.

- ⮩ You have identified the processes that exist within these roles (these are split into single and multi role processes).

- ⮩ You have highlighted the areas that you are concerned with the most, and shortlisted these to be worked on first.

- ⮩ You have mapped out one of the key processes, identified issues and tweaked them.

- ⮩ You have included staff members where possible to ensure buy-in.

- ⮩ You have allocated steps to each role and considered the link between them.

## PART 2: Implementing *'The System'* Into Your Business

You need to make these systems accessible to your employees, if they don't know where they are, or have difficulty finding them, they won't be used.

Of course if you have existing staff, and they have helped you develop the systems, you can get them to help further by linking the documents or adapting existing forms or processes.

### How to store these files

A good tip is to set up a *'Systems Folder'* within your *'Document Store'* (*see Chapter 4 for more information on this*) to store these systems.

- • If you have departments, then it can be useful to sub-divide the folder into departments, and then put a *Manuals Folder* in each department.

- The '*Manuals Folder*' is where you will save your systems.

- If you have mapped a system that involves many departments, then save each part of the system in the relevant department's manual, e.g. the Sales Department, or you can just save the systems in the folder called '*Processes.*'

- I would also recommend printing your manual out and have it lying around, even if it's not finished. If it's lying around the office, you can refer to it regularly.

- Another tip for making the systems accessible is using dual screens, and encouraging employees to have the system open when they are doing work.

- Finally, check out http://www.sweetprocess.com/ for a Cloud-based solution for systemising. This really is a great tool, allowing you to add videos; links and a whole lot more.

## Getting your staff on board

In your journey to implement the systems approach, there will inevitably come a time where you can't get the staff to buy into the systems. It's much easier if you have had their help with the initial mapping, but even then, when the initial mapping process is complete you may find it hard to get employees to actually follow the systems.

Often, ironically, when I go back into a company after a few months and review where we are on the journey to a fully systemised business, and I talk to employees, I often find that it's the business owner to blame if things are slipping – and as you know, you are responsible for everything that goes wrong in your business.

What I often find is that the system is coming along nicely, but the owner, or someone else who is key in the business, thinks and demonstrates that these systems don't apply to them, and undermines the whole thing. Even if they agree in principle, when it comes to actually doing it, they fail to follow the systems.

> Systems need to be part of the culture of the business, and you have to buy into them at least 50% more than your employees. If you have a manager, they need to be 50% more bought-in than their subordinates.

When something goes wrong, you need to be heard to be saying, *"Let's review the system,"* not *"Whose fault was that"* If someone asks how to do something, you should say, *"Let's take a look at the system first".*

As mentioned above, inclusion of your team in the building of the systems is the biggest single, most contributory factor to getting them to follow the processes. By allowing them input in the sculpting, designing and writing of the process you will get more buy-in.

## Overcoming obstacles with the 'Four-Step Process'

Let's say you have identified a change to a system that will massively improve how your business works, and you now need to make the change with the person doing the role.

The problem is that you are now going to attempt to make a change to someone's behaviour, if you have employed someone for any length of time you will know that this can be a challenge.

To make a system change that sticks with an employee, whether it is a new employee or an existing one, there is a *four-step process that I have discovered:*

1. **Run through the details of the system** with the employees that will use it

2. **Demonstrate the system** practically, and work together to find any flaws.

3. Now ask them to **follow it** with you observing, testing it to see if it succeeds.

4. **Follow up** by reviewing it on points two and three at least once a month for three months.

*Let's look at this in more detail:*

## 1. Run through the details of the system

Introduce the system to the employee, read them through it line by and line, and consider what the system is trying to achieve. If it's a simple system this won't take long, but if it's a more complex one, take some real time over it.

If the process involves a number of people across departments, get them all together in the room and talk it through.

Allow them to talk about potential issues, but be on the lookout for anyone with personal hang-ups trying to influence a system. If you see a personal hang up, then you need to deal with it head on, as you may have the wrong person in the role.

### A Real Life Example

An example of this occurred with a client of mine when we introduced a process to follow up the quotes produced by the business. The person doing the role at the time was not comfortable talking to customers on the phone, and because of this, they wouldn't use the system of calling back their potential customers to ask if the quote was okay, and if they wanted to place an order. Ultimately, it was decided that this person was working in the wrong role, as it interfered with the system that was set in place for the call back procedure, and they were then moved to a more suitable one.

## 2. Demonstrate the *system* practically

Once you have talked through the system, follow it practically with the person doing the role, and go through everything it tells you to do. A system that sounds great in theory can fall apart when the reality of actually doing it is tested. A system that says you must make 50 calls a day sounds great, but needs testing to see if this can actually be done. At this point, there may be tweaks needed.

If this throws up any issues then re-visit the system and amend it. Perhaps ask the staff member to do it.

## 3. Follow it

Once you have gone through it with them, (and possibly tweaked it) allow them to run through it on their own and observe, giving pointers where necessary, just to make sure they are comfortable with the process.

## 4. Review it

Don't leave them alone for too long, go back to the system and review how it's going. Check they are happy or to see if the system needs changing. Do this regularly, and if you discover major variations start the process over again.

*Just to reiterate, as this is vital, when you implement any new systems to ensure they stick:*

- ✓ Run through the system with the employees that will use it.

- ✓ Practically demonstrate the system and together find any flaws.

- ✓ Now ask them to follow it with you observing, and actually test to see if it succeeds.

- ✓ Follow up on points two and three at least once a month for three months.

If this sounds like a lot of effort, then you're right, but it's also the most effective way of getting a system into use and to keep it being used.

In the very good book, *'Leadership and the one minute manager,'* Ken Blanchard *et al.* describe a management style of *'leave alone zap'* – hiring a new employee, showing them around and then leaving them alone, expecting them to do a good job, and then we zap (reprimand) them when they don't. This leaves the employee dejected and is a poor management style.

This is the same as giving a system to an employee, and expecting them to follow it without the steps above. Just showing a new system and announcing this is how we are going to do it now isn't going to make it work, you have to work the system into their role.

### Real Life Example

I once spent days with a client writing a system for a sales meeting. We researched the past results; we brainstormed, and came up with what we thought was a killer system. It was brilliant. We even tried it out on real customers, and it worked every time.

We then rolled it out to the sales staff; we talked it through with them, overcame their objections, made some amendments and let them go. Job done, or so we thought. Six months later the MD did a ride along with a salesperson, and he was appalled that the system we had spent hours developing, was not being used.

The salesperson couldn't explain why he wasn't following the system, he had just got out of the habit, and sales suffered as a result. The reason the system hadn't stuck was we had broken the golden rules; we hadn't practically demonstrated it and we had left it too long to follow up.

**TOP TIP:** *The Outgoing Employee.* A quick word about outgoing employees. It is a big mistake to allow the outgoing employee to train the *incoming* employee. The outgoing employee will have developed, despite all of your training, their own way of doing things. By allowing the outgoing employee to train the incoming one, you miss the opportunity to re-enforce the systems and to get back to where the roles should be.

So for all new employees at the heavily systems-orientated induction, follow the *four steps above* on every system to ensure that the role is done how you want it to be done.

It's a fact that new employees are far more likely to accept and follow the systems than old employees because they readily accept the culture of the organisation they are joining; they accept that this is how things are done here. By allowing your old employees to train your new employees, you aren't enforcing how you want it done, instead you could be teaching them old habits.

The old employee will say stuff like, *"They want you to fill this in, but I never bother,"* or *"We are supposed to do it like this but…"*

For practical reasons you may have to use the outgoing employee and if you do make sure you have run through the system with them before the new employee starts.

## To summarise:

This was a huge chapter and we covered a lot of ground!

*Here is a summary to recap:*

**PART 1: The practical benefits of a systemised business:**

- ✓ Increased efficiency from day one – new employees are empowered to do the role as they have systems to follow.

✓ Reduce errors – errors are learnt from, repeated mistakes minimised.

✓ The ability to expand and scale your business.

✓ Peace of mind – if you put a system in place correctly, then you can relax knowing that the job will be done and you can delegate in confidence. Delegating with confidence is one of the biggest challenges managers and owners face – systems help with this.

✓ Freedom – it sounds dramatic, but systems = freedom from the business for the owners. Freedom to do what you want, you may want to carry on working in the business or leave it to run on its own, but a fully systemised business will allow you the choice.

**PART 2: Implementing the systems into your business:**

✓ Identify the roles that exist in your business – these are split between individual and shared roles.

✓ Identify the key processes that exist in the business – these are split between single-role processes and multi-role processes.

✓ Map out the key processes in the business starting from a high level – start with the sales process.

✓ Add more detail to the process, initially just brainstorming but then in a more structured way.

✓ Now identify which roles match which process.

✓ Think carefully how these roles interact with each other within the process – how you are going to link the roles.

✓ When implementing a system use the four rules to make sure it sticks – don't just show an employee the system and expect them to follow it.

If you can take one thing from this chapter it's that you need to be working on your business to create a business that does not rely on you. The only way to do this is to systemise it.

If you want to do some more reading around the systems approach I *highly recommend: The E-Myth Revisited* – Michael Gerber and *Work the System: The Simple Mechanics of Making More & Working Less* - Sam Carpenter (full details are in the *Reference* section page 192)

> *"Once you recognize that the purpose of your life is not to serve your business, but that the primary purpose of your business is to serve your life, you can then go to work on your business, rather than in it, with a full understanding of why it is absolutely necessary for you to do so."*
> **Michael Gerber - The E-myth**

# Chapter 4: The Organised Computer

*"A computer will do what you tell it to do, but that may be much different from what you had in mind."*
**Joseph Weizenbaum**

Like it or not we all have computers in our home, in the office, on our person and soon, apparently, on our wrist or in a pair of glasses.

The computer and Internet have been responsible for as much change in small business as the loom in the textile industry in pre-industrial Britain. Almost every business has a computer, and every business relies on it to do a big chunk of the work within it.

The clue for one of the biggest issues with a PC is in its name – *Personal Computer.*

They are designed for an individual to work and find things on, not for a small business where lots of different people all use the same machine (or server). This makes them a potential organisational trap for your business that many small business owners fall into.

This chapter is all about getting a system going on your PCs or Macs that makes files easy to find, and ensures they are safely backed up.

It's also about getting the most out of the *Internet for your business.*

## The Tale of Two Brothers

**John** started off with a laptop, which he used to raise all his sales invoices, store all his quotes, and where he kept a spreadsheet he had been given from his accountant for his bookkeeping.

To save documents, he either used the *'My Documents'* folder or saved things to the desktop. He either let the computer name the files for him, or he picked some random names for files.

When he took on a new employee in the office, he bought them a laptop, and they used the same approach as he did, although he did get an IT person to ensure that the 'My Documents' folder could be seen by each laptop so that files could be shared.

The system grew along these lines for quite some time, but problems arose when a third and fourth employee came along. The major issue was finding files.

Files were saved in more than one location, and each person had their own default text style and naming convention (the way they named and saved the file).

This bedlam was fine when it was just John, but as the business grew, it caused all sort of issues, the biggest one being the amount of time it took to find anything.

In addition, John had a disconnected business – he used standalone software and applications for everything. Duplication of effort was everywhere; his pricing package didn't talk to his accountancy package, his time sheets were done manually on paper, and there was time wasted at every stage of the business.

**Stephen**, on the other hand, had a different approach. At first, he still used his one laptop, but instead of using 'My

Documents,' he set up one folder (*'Document Store'*) to save everything in and then made sure that this folder was backed up.

In this folder, he set up sub folders, including a folder for customers. Each customer had a folder that contained anything relevant to that customer.

Stephen resisted the temptation for having a quote folder, or an invoice folder; instead he saved these into the customer folder. He maintained a list of quotes and sales invoices separately.

Stephen synced this folder using Box.net so that he knew everything was backed up. When the time came to expand and take on staff, Stephen shared this one folder and made the rule that no documents would be saved in any place, other than the main folder (in its correct place).

Eventually he bought a file server, then a small business server, but he never lost the central storage idea.

He put in some further rules for this folder such as a universal naming convention for all the files, so they were easily recognisable and above all, discoverable!

The key thing here is that the way this was all set up made it *scalable*. The business could not outgrow this system.

Stephen had a connected business. He used the Internet as a basis for his software needs. His pricing package linked to his accountancy package and this all linked to his Customer Relationship Management Database (CRM). Duplication did exist in the system, but it was to a minimum. Stephen's staff did their time sheets directly via a third party application, so no paper was used and there was no typing up of timesheets to worry about.

This timesheet application linked to his bookkeeping package to automatically record the costs of his employees' time.

# How You Can Organise Your Computer

## *Organising electronic files*

This is what you need to do to set up this computer filing structure in your business. The aim is to create a place where all documents are saved, are accessible, and most importantly, allow the system to be scalable.

Create a folder on your C Drive, server or Cloud-based archive called '*Document Store,*' or a name of your choice, and make it available to all staff.

Everything in your business will be saved into this main file. If you want HR and Finance in a separate file with separate permissions, then simply create two new folders and store them on the C Drive (see the tabbed examples on next page)

In the main *Document Store*, create another file called '*Customers,*' and then have a folder broken down alphabetically, e.g. A – G, H – M, etc. Under each heading have a customer folder.

For example, a customer might be Bexley Council. Make a folder called Bexley Council, and in *this* customer folder you could have a folder called '*Jobs*'. In here you would put each job you are given by the customer, and you would have a folder for '*Quotes*', '*Orders*', etc.

Save your documents (Word, Excel etc.) in the following naming convention **YYYY.MM.DD.FILENAME**

Now that may sound confusing, but the result will look something like this: (See next page)

*How long do you think it would take me to find the Bexley quote in a hurry?*

In addition, formatting the date like this: *YYYY.MM.DD Filename* means that all documents are listed in order, by date. This enables you to quickly see which document is the most recent.

*Other folders under your document store could include:*

- ➲ Marketing – a place for your marketing material.
- ➲ Systems - a place for your procedures
- ➲ Products - a place for details of products.
- ➲ Human Resources.
- ➲ Finance.

**Once you have built this document store, there are two *key rules* to follow:**

1. Keep everything in it; don't allow anyone to save anything to their desktop or to their C drive. All documents should be in document store. If they wish to keep personal stuff on your system then set up a personal file on your document store (perhaps make a folder called Staff, and then named folders within that).

2.  Get a backup system in place, either in the Cloud, or if it's a physical disk make sure you keep one backup disk off-site at all times for security. Make it one person's responsibility to take the backup drive home with them each night.

Here is an example of a skeleton completed Document store:

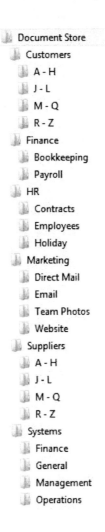

To help you, I have created a ready made set up *Document Store*. To get a copy,  simply visit: **book.theorganisedbusiness.co.uk**

## 'The Cloud'

Your document store doesn't need to be on a physical server or PC at all, it can be stored virtually on *'The Cloud'*. The number of Cloud-based storage systems for files are steadily increasing. Here are a few that are prominent at the moment.

### Dropbox

Dropbox offers a free and paid service that lets you bring your photos, docs, and videos anywhere and share them easily. Never email yourself a file again! *www.dropbox.com*

To get the most out of it, it's worth paying for as the free account has limited storage space.

Dropbox can be accessed via the web or downloaded onto your computer.  When downloaded, it sets up a folder near your C drive that allows you to access and back up files without logging on to the website.

Arguably Dropbox is the most popular of the cloud storage solutions.

### Box.net

Box lets you store all of your content online, so you can access, manage and share it from anywhere. It can be integrated with a number of third party services such as Google Apps and Salesforce and accessed on mobile devices. *www.box.net*

Box has a number of other features such as assigning task-related files to others.

*Others worth considering are:*

✓   Live Drive - www.livedrive.co.uk

- ✓ Google Drive - https://drive.google.com/
- ✓ Amazon Cloud Storage - https://www.amazon.com/clouddrive
- ✓ Apple iCloud - www.apple.com/uk/icloud/
- ✓ Microsoft One Drive - www.onedrive.com

### *Completely in 'The Cloud'*

Some businesses now choose to use these services entirely and not save a single thing on their office-based systems.

The upside of this is that the files are available everywhere there is an Internet connection, and in theory should be safe and secure.

The downside is, that in some cases, they are not available when there is no Internet connection, although some of these do offer an off-line mode that can still be accessed on your PC, and will then sync when your connection returns.

# Spreadsheets, Spreadsheets and More Spreadsheets

If you have never used a spreadsheet in your life, then you are missing out on one of the *best tools* for organisation and analysis ever invented.

The spreadsheet, be it Google docs, Smartsheet, Supercal, Excel or Lotus Calc, is one of the most versatile tools for analysing data.

Spreadsheets can be easily set up and used for any data. Here are five spreadsheet ideas that could be of use to your business.

**A quote spreadsheet** that lists everything you have quoted, with three tabs, one for quotes, one for ordered and one for fulfilled. A simple macro can move the job across from one tab to another to help track your work.

**A transport organizer** that has all your vehicles on it, that tells you when you are nearing a key date, the MOT date, and insurance renewal or tax renewal.

**A staff holiday planner** that helps you track holidays.

**A pricing sheet** that helps you calculate prices – a simple costs plus sheet that you enter costs or a time-based overhead model. Once set up, you will be pricing in seconds rather than hours.

**A cash forecasting sheet** to forecast cash for up to eight weeks in the future, and tell you if you are going to run out of cash. (See *Chapter 7 – Organise your cash* for more info)

---

 If you think some of these spreadsheets might be of use to your business then why not download these for **FREE,** simply by visiting **book.theorganisedbusiness.co.uk**

---

### Don't just read it, *do it!*

There are also loads of templates available within software programs. For example, Microsoft Excel has an amazing array of pre-formatted sheets that may be of use to you. Also, if you are not familiar with Excel, or any other of these other spreadsheet software solutions, then there are lots of books available that will get you started. It really is worth taking a look, and implementing these types of files into your business.

*One word of warning about spreadsheets* – they can easily contain errors that cause you problems going forward, and they aren't necessarily the best tools for scalability, but you will need to use them to some extent in your business, so it is well worth getting to know how they work.

## Email

Email is a staple now of most if not all businesses, and is 100% essential, but it can also be a distraction from the day-to-day activities.

The way you sort your inbox could have a massive impact on how efficiently you use email. In Graham Allcotts book, *'How to be a Productivity Ninja',* he has a whole section dedicated to *getting your inbox to zero!* Well worth a read.

One option is to set up rules, so that emails are diverted either to folders for processing later, or for other members of your team to pick up.

Our system is to have a folder for every customer, and for us the save the emails into that folder. This makes it much easier to find things when we are in a hurry.

There is software available now for team sharing of emails. The way this works is that emails from all staff are funnelled through a third party application and then this software sorts your email. The reason that this is important, is if there is a multi role and more than one person is responsible for a role, say customer service, the software ensures that emails aren't missed and other members of the team can see what has been said on the email chain.

The other thing we do is to forward important emails to our Customer Relationship Management Database (CRM), so they are recorded against customers.

## The Connected Business

A connected business is one where the software in the business is connected or joined, where data entered into one piece of software is updated across all the software in the business automatically. This removes the necessity for re-typing standing data more than once, and reduces the possibility of error and mistakes. A side effect of this is increased efficiency and more time, and suddenly another barrier for scalability is removed as the business can deal with vast amounts of data easily.

A few years ago, the thought of a connected business, one where the software in the business connects to other software to avoid manual duplication of data entered, was a pipe dream limited to medium or large businesses, but the Internet and SAAS (Software As A Service) have completely changed the game. SAAS is a subscription-based model, where software is available to use via the web for a fraction of the cost of buying it.

As well as the benefits of always having the latest version, and of it being available from any PC, SAAS has the bonus of an API (Application Programme Interface) which means that the software can talk to other software. The designers of the software have opened a universal channel for other developers to connect their software.

In the past, this would have been a bespoke development job costing thousands, now the work is done for you, which means you can build your own suite of tools for your business, all connected, for a relatively low monthly fee.

So your website can talk to your accounts package, your CRM – database can talk to your accounts package and your email campaign manager is updated by your website. In the past these would all have been standalone packages that would have needed to be manually updated individually, slowing you down and increasing the possibility of error.

### Real Life Example

Accsys Accountants are a Gold Partner with bookkeeping software called Xero. Xero has changed the way that bookkeeping for small businesses works forever. The only issue is that small businesses haven't fully realised it yet.

Xero has halved the time it takes to do your books over traditional bookkeeping software. It's intuitive, and easy to use, with a bunch of extra features such as the ability to link to your bank, and to email your invoices and statements directly to customers, so no more keying in data.

Xero takes this further; it allows you to automatically email customer invoices each month, using a standard email, along with a link so they can pay them directly via PayPal or other providers.

Xero also has an API; it can be connected to other intuitive software.

*How does this all help?*

Imagine two businesses with online shops, one uses Xero with its linked API, and one does not.

In the shop with Xero, every time an item is sold via the shop, an invoice (receipt) is raised and posted in Xero. When the customer pays, the information is posted via the bank or PayPal into Xero. The only thing the user has to do is reconcile, which Xero has made very easy to do.

The other business has to manually raise the invoice in their bookkeeping software, manually key in the bank information, and manually reconcile. This massively increases the chance of error, reduces the ability of the business to scale, and worst of all takes unnecessary time.

The time savings that can be made by having a connected business, demonstrated in this example, work for all kinds of businesses, for businesses with CRM databases, physical epos systems, people who run a business with time sheets, garages, property companies. The list goes on. Xero has a bunch of Add-on partners that it works with to provide solutions to common problems.

*Go to www.xero.com* and click more and Add ons.

**SOFTWARE TIP:** If you use online software, and you are curious as to what other software could connect with yours, check out *https://zapier.com/* This site gives you some idea of online software that can be connected together. Generally the rule is if it's web based it can be connected.

Once final thing on **SAAS** – *Software as a Service*, any software that is online that doesn't give you a free 30 day free trial or similar, should be avoided. Most software companies will give a free trial because they are confident you will like the product and keep paying.

## To summarise:

- Don't use your *'My Documents'* to save your files.

- Make sure all documents are saved in a *central document storage area* as outlined.

- Make sure this central area is the *only* place documents and files are saved and make sure it is backed up regularly.

- Implement some rules for this such as the naming of files with this format yyyy.mm.dd filename.

- Consider cloud backup and storage.

- Don't shy away from spreadsheets they are a valuable tool for any business.

- Consider ditching software downloaded onto your PC for a cloud-based alternative – this software is always up to date, accessible from anywhere and most importantly can be connected to other software avoiding duplication.

# Chapter 5: Organise Your Sales And Marketing

*"Marketing is not an event, but a process . . . It has a beginning, a middle, but never an end, for it is a process. You improve it, perfect it, change it, even pause it. But you never stop it completely."*
**Jay Conrad Levinson**

This is a huge topic, and it is beyond the scope of this book to go into too much depth, but hopefully I can give you some pointers that will help you set up a solid *sales and marketing plan.*

Firstly, let's define the differences between **sales** and **marketing.** Broadly speaking, *marketing is everything that you do to reach and persuade prospects,* and *sales is everything that you do to close the sale and get a signed agreement or contract.*

In other words, marketing is about lead generation activities, and sales is about turning leads into sales.

Sales is a numbers game, the more prospects you find, the more meetings you can have, the more meetings, the better chance of a sale. The idea is to increase your percentages in all the categories, and having a systemised approach can go a long way to doing this. An organised approach to sales will allow you to increase the leads through your sales funnel, to qualify the leads, and to prepare for the sales meeting that will increase your sales success.

The same can be said of marketing, an organised approach will help you massively increase the amount of leads it can generate.

## The Tale of Two Brothers

**John** didn't have a marketing plan, his marketing was a bit hit or miss; he spent a lot of money on advertising, but wasn't sure how effective it was. He didn't measure his success in any one activity; he just tended to go with his gut instinct on what worked.

He stopped marketing when things got busy because he was afraid of new leads. New leads led to extra work in pricing and quoting etc. John's turnover was a bit erratic, as he only increased his marketing activities when things got slow. This had a knock-on effect on cash flow by making it difficult to forecast.

John felt he was wasting a lot of money on ineffective marketing activities, but he didn't know what to do about it.

John didn't have sales meetings with customers, (well at least he didn't recognise them as such) instead he let potential customers call him, and he went around to measure up. He made no attempt to prepare for the meeting, other than to make sure he had his tape measure. He didn't research whom he was meeting and made no attempt to improve the way the meeting went.

For these reasons, Johns' chance of closing the sale was unpredictable. John realised that he needed a salesperson because he wasn't the best at it, so he employed one. He didn't really give the salesperson any guidance, he just let them get on with it; he didn't systemise the role or show the salesperson where they fitted in.

The salesperson didn't really work out for John as he didn't get it, he didn't buy into the ethos, or understand the business. Instead he did it his way, and did everything he could to get the sale, but not necessarily the way John wanted to do it.

This caused John a few problems as he wouldn't dream of pressurising customers, but his salespeople had targets and no guidance, so inevitably they put prospective customers under pressure.

**Stephen**, on the other hand, had a plan for his marketing. He knew how many leads he needed for his business, and through a process of testing and measuring; he knew what worked and what didn't.

He knew which activities he needed to spend on to increase his leads. Stephen didn't waste a lot of money on ineffective marketing.

In addition, Stephen developed a sales system that he tested and tested in his sales meetings, until he had perfected the approach. Along the way, he wrote it down, and when he had perfected it, he ensured this was recorded.

He thought about how his new sales system linked to other parts of the business.

Stephen then hired a salesperson, and followed the four rules for implementing a system. He trained the salesperson on the system, worked through the system with the salesperson and then watched them as they performed the tasks necessary, making sure to debrief regularly. Eventually, Stephen allowed the salesperson to go out on his own, but he didn't just leave him to it, he followed up with him regularly.

Stephen followed this approach with each salesperson he hired. Using this method, he got consistent results from his sales team. He knew this because he measured those results and also emailed every customer with a questionnaire to get feedback.

If an individual salesperson's figures dropped Stephen went out with them and reviewed their work.

Stephen realised that you could increase your sales if you constantly reviewed the processes, and practised a few preparation techniques before the sales.

## The Organised Marketing Approach

A lot of money can be wasted on marketing. There are numerous approaches you can try to generate new leads; here I list 10 ideas that you could try later, with some comments from me. Whatever you do in marketing, I suggest you do some preliminary planning before you even start.

Four **key questions** to ask yourself before you begin:

1. Who are you trying to reach?

2. What action do you want them to take when you reach them?

3. How much are you willing to spend on each new lead?

4. How are you going to measure this activity to see that it is effective?

### 1. Who are you trying to reach?

Being able to describe your customer in detail is important, if you want to choose the correct method of reaching them. If, for example, you were targeting accountants, then you wouldn't advertise in a local newspaper as it's far too generalised. This would be untargeted marketing, because most of the people you would reach wouldn't be accountants. It would be far better to advertise in a trade magazine. Equally, if you want to set up a stall at an exhibition, it's probably best not to go to a general business exhibition; instead you would go to one targeted specifically to accountants.

This is obvious stuff, but you would be surprised how many people just chuck an advert in the local paper, without asking themselves who will read it or who they want as customers.

## 2. What action do you want them to take when you reach them?

The methods of marketing you choose should have a desired response or call to action. If you call up your target customer, what results do you want from this call?

Marketing tailored to a desired outcome is more effective than a general approach, especially when the budget is low.

What action do you want your customer to take when they respond to your marketing? To call you, to visit your showroom or sign up for your newsletter?

## 3. How much are you willing to spend on each new lead?

How much is each new customer worth to you? If you spent £500, but achieved two new customers, is that something you would keep doing, or would you stop? If you spent £1000 and achieved one customer, would you continue that activity?

By calculating the amount you are willing to spend to win each new customer, you are on the way to setting a marketing budget, and you will know if an activity meets that criterion.

Let's say you spend £500 a month over a three-month period, and it gets you one customer. You would probably think you had wasted your money and stop that activity, but if that customer is worth £20,000 to you, then you might make the decision to carry on, or even up the budget.

## 4. How are you going to measure this activity to see that it's effective?

Whatever marketing activities you choose you will need to organise and measure them. I suggest you start a spreadsheet, a tracker to list all the activities you are undertaking, and how much they are costing. Then for each activity measure the response. For some methods, it will be easier to measure response, such as pay per click web advertising. For others, you might need to be creative. For example, on your adverts you could have a dedicated phone number to call or even just a code to present for a discount.

Whatever the method of collecting data, you must measure the response so you can make informed decisions about what is working. Enter this onto your tracker and compare the relative value of each lead generation's activity

### The marketing calendar

Another option to track and organise your marketing is a *'marketing calendar'*, which sets out your annual marketing activities. If your marketing activities change depending on the season, then the marketing calendar is a great way to map seasonal activities.

 It doesn't matter what your marketing spreadsheet looks like as long as you have one, if you want a pointer there is a template available for free just visit **book.theorganisedbusiness.co.uk** and download it.

### Testing

Whatever marketing activity you decide to try, you need to make sure you don't overspend on one form of marketing in isolation. To do this could potentially waste time and money on an ineffective approach. A better approach is to test each activity carefully, and measure the response before investing in more of the activity.

## Marketing approaches

Here are **10 approaches** to marketing that you could try, along with some comments from me.

### 1. Advertising

You can spend thousands on advertising and never get results, but by following these simple rules, you can maximise your marketing spend on advertising.

- Test it small first - pick an area and a publication and try it out.

- Once you have tested the location, try testing the page your advert appears on, the size of your advert, your offer, the size of the headline on the advert.

- Think about the impact of the main copy, should you make the telephone number bigger, or change the colours etc.?

- Offer the customer something, maybe 10% off or a FREE offer?

- Include a code to help you measure the response.

### 2. Trade Shows and Exhibitions

These can be expensive, but also can be effective. If you are local, go to local events. If you have a national customer base then find the most targeted event.

- You don't always have to exhibit at events, just go along and chat to people and hand out cards. Be careful not to sell too hard to exhibitors on their own stands as they came to sell to you, but a bit of networking never hurts.

- If you are exhibiting, talk to as many people as possible, don't judge by appearance. If the exhibition operates a bar scanner system, get one and scan as many people in as possible.

- Plan your activities, if you are sending a team then spread them out and give them tasks to complete. Exhibitions are generally short so you have to maximise your opportunity in a limited time window.

- If you send someone on your behalf, make sure they understand what to do. Make sure they approach people that pass your stand and draw potential customers to your business.

- Make sure your stand is simple and approachable, and that it lets potential customers know what you do.

The worst sin I see at exhibitions is exhibitors waiting to be spoken to. This seems ridiculous to me, as they've paid a lot of money to be there, so if you decide to show at one, maximise the opportunity you have, and actively speak to potential clients and don't be a shrinking violet.

If you can get interviewed or give a talk on a topic at the exhibition, do it – it will raise your profile.

### 3. Existing Customers

Assuming you provide a great service, then past customers are your most valuable contacts because you have an existing relationship with them. Nurture that relationship, keep in contact and don't let them fade away. In short, find a way of selling to your existing customers.

- Most businesses waste the opportunity to stay in contact with their existing customers. Most businesses ignore existing customers, and focus their efforts on looking for new customers. This is an error.

- New customers are much harder to come by than existing ones. Why not stay in contact with these customers by sending offers, calling or emailing them? Get permission to do this by offering an incentive but make sure you do it.

- Also, why not ask existing customers if there is anything else they would like you to offer them. You never know; they may just give you an idea for a new range.

- If you have done a good job, just ask for a recommendation. Offer them a discount on future orders if they do. Make it easy for them to refer you – send them some business cards.

- Once they have referred you, send them a thank you in the form of a note, or a small gift etc.

This works for most types of business, from a cake shop to a car garage.

---

### Real Life Example

My local cake shop offers a cake maker's loyalty scheme, whereby you pay a nominal annual sum of £25 or so, to receive offers and invitations in the post. This scheme works on many levels, not least to stay in contact with existing customers and build brand loyalty. It also allows them to increase sales by issuing offers as and when required.

Could *you* offer your existing customers a membership or loyalty scheme?

One of the services Accsys Accountants offers is Xero conversion and training. We help businesses get on to and get the most out of this market leading bookkeeping software. Not all of these businesses become clients of Accsys Accountants but I have introduced a great way of staying in contact with them: *The Accsys Xero User Support Group*. This is not just an e-mail group for anyone using Xero but also for anyone we have converted and trained.

This enables me to create a win win situation I can keep in contact with these potential customers and they get help, tips and advice delivered to their inbox.

## 4. Direct Mail

Direct mail is a much-maligned form of marketing that, whilst a little old fashioned, can still work for many businesses. The key thing to consider is getting your mailing list correct and up-to date, getting your content correct and testing it small.

Direct mail is a low response media, as it will only work if it lands at the point of time, that a person is looking for your product or service. Therefore, in terms of return for pounds spent it is fairly low. However, if you keep costs down and test approaches until you find one that works, then direct mail can be effective.

An approach that you may find works is to use a mailing house; these will print, pack and post your direct mail for you and can even save you money in postage as they buy in bulk. They will definitely save you time, but can be expensive. Mailing houses do not just have to be for large quantity mail outs they will also consider small runs.

Direct mail is much less effective than it used to be, but if it is targeted, and well thought out it can still work.

Direct mail response rates increase if followed up by a phone call.

## 5. Pay Per Click Campaigns

Pay per click advertising has been pioneered by Google and is an excellent targeted marketing campaign. It works by you setting up an advert on Google, to drive traffic to your website. You are only charged for this advert when someone clicks on it. You set a budget, what key words the advert will appear on, and when and where it appears.

This is a cost-effective alternative to traditional advertising as it is targeted to specific Google searches, such as accountants in Maidstone. Your advert appears to the right, or the top of the Google search results as a sponsored link.

However, you are in competition with other advertisers who may appear first if they have set their budget higher than yours.

*Other things to consider*

- Be careful that the costs of the campaign aren't more than you can afford to budget, and watch the response carefully.

- One of the best methods of maximising pay per click, is to get the link you post on the advert to go to a landing page, that offers the customer some information in exchange for their email address, e.g. a free report or e-book.

- To see examples of how this works, search Google for different types of services, and see where the sponsored links take you.

**For example if I search for *Car Ports* on Google:**

(See screen shot on next page) I get 35 million results, the top one being a **PPC advert**. If I click on this link, the page I get taken to is a landing page (second screen shot)

*Google Search results*

*The landing page I get taken to, when I click the first option.*

This is a landing page that has a wealth of information including the offer of a FREE guide in exchange for my email address.

This website is only for people looking for information on this topic, and this is exactly what it offers.

The result of this PPC campaign is the receipt of the email addresses of interested prospective customers to whom they have demonstrated that they are experts in this field. They can now be targeted, in the hope that they will convert into customers after a few follow up emails.

Outsourcing PPC is an increasingly popular service. If you do choose to do this, then you will be asked how much your budget is each month. When doing this, make sure you find out how much will be spent on the actual PPC, and how much the fee is. Some PPC companies have been known to take up to 75% of your budget as the fee!

### 6.  Search Engine Optimisation

SEO is basically free web advertising. By optimising your web page for specific searches made by individuals, and getting incoming links into your page, you can drive your site to the top of Google searches.

Google is very clever; it reviews and ranks every website submitted to it, and knows what your content is. Also, Google ranks your website for the importance on that subject. When someone searches a specific subject, it looks at the content and also the importance of the site.

The person who designs your website should know about SEO, but may not necessarily. Ask them, and if they don't, you may have to educate them on the subject or hire someone who is a specialist in the subject.

These are the basic ways you should ensure your website is optimised, but there are whole books on this subject, (a great example is *The Lazy Website Syndrome* by Tony Messer and Pilar Torres Wahlberg) so we won't go into too much detail here.

### Keywords

Include your keywords, the words people will use to search for your particular trade or service:

- Your page content. Make sure your text is interesting, informative and appealing, and ensure that your keywords are included, but also take care to avoid over using them, as the content still needs to be useable.

- Your page title. This is the title at the top of your page in blue. This is the headline listing on Google.

- Images. Images can have tags attached to them called an ALT tag. These have default names as to what that image may be called e.g. 'man in suit'. The names of all the images with an ALT tag on your website should be changed to those containing your key words; ensure that your web designer knows this.

## Site Map

A site map helps Google find all your pages quickly and easily, by laying out exactly what you have on your site. A site map can be made simply, by creating a page that links to all other pages on your site, with easy to read headings. A good website that easily allows you to create your SiteMap can be found at http://www.xml-sitemaps.com/

## Link Building

Links, in this context, are one way links to your website from other websites. This shows Google how important your web page is. Broadly speaking, a page with a 100 quality incoming links is more important to Google than one with 10 links.

Where can you get incoming links?

- Your customers - If your customers have websites, it would be worth asking them if they could put a link on their website that links to yours.

- Your suppliers - If you can leverage anyone then it's your suppliers. Tell them that you have been their customer for some time, and you would appreciate it if they could put a link on their website that links back to yours.

- Directories - There are hundreds of online directories, some paid, and many free ones. Upload your company description to an online directory and include a link back to your website. Simply go to Google and search for relevant directories for your particular business or niche. Don't ignore the local directories such as:

- Google Places
- Yahoo Local

- Article Directories - submitting articles to online article directories has become very popular for SEO purposes.

  The idea is that you write a 300 - 400 word article about your business/area of expertise, and submit that article to an online directory such as *www.ezinearticles.com*, then at the bottom of that article place a link back to your website.

  As the article is original content relevant to your business, and as it is part of a website that contains millions of pages, it can be seen as a very good link to your website and that is what Google likes.

- You can also get incoming links by leaving posts or comments on forums etc. as long as you include a link back to your website.

## Internal Links

SEO can be improved by creating a link from each page of your site to the front page of your website. This makes it easier for users and Google to navigate your website.

Finally make sure, if possible, that links include your keywords. For example, instead of saying: For information on diamond rings click here, say: For information on diamond rings click – Diamond Rings.

## Testimonials on website

Testimonials, reviews, and recommendations are a powerful thing. Customers like to see what other people have said about you. The most powerful ones are the ones that you have no control over, where a customer can review your service, for example, the feedback option on eBay.

Second to that are testimonials you receive from your customers.

- The first step is to ask for a testimonial from all your existing customers. If you use a feedback form, add a box that says, *"Please tick this box if you do not want us to add your details as a testimonial"*.

- Otherwise, design a form and write a list of testimonials comments that you would want your customers to say about you, and email your customers to ask them if they would be happy to put their name to any of them, or even write their own?

- Once you have them, use them on every piece of marketing you have. On your mail shots, emails, brochures, leaflets and website. Have a dedicated page for testimonials, and dot them around your site.

- Ask for reviews from your customers on Google – set up a Google plus page for your business and then ask your customers to leave a review on there.

**A warning** about SEO techniques, *do not* attempt to trick Google with SEO – the basic rule is that if you are making your website easier to use, more relevant and better for the visitors, the better Google will rank it. For Google, **content is king** - the more relevant the content on your website the better.

## 7. Telemarketing

If it is done with tact and is targeted in the right way, telemarketing can be very effective.

- Produce a script so you know what is being said, and specify exactly what you want out of it. Do you want an appointment or are you just gathering information?

- Test the script to make sure it works, and at that point consider outsourcing it.

- The thing to remember with Telemarketing, is that if you are doing it yourself, don't take the rejection personally, you will get a lot of no's before you get a yes, and whatever you do don't give up – it's a numbers game.

## 8.  Email Marketing

Email marketing is emerging as an alternative to direct mail, with the advantage that it is cheap to produce and follow up. Be careful though, as people can be sensitive to it, and there are laws against spamming, but as long as you have an opt-out clause on your email and you don't send unsolicited emails, you should be fine.

Keep all your customers on an email distribution list, so you can keep in contact with them for marketing purposes. Devise a method of collecting the email addresses, and ways of getting customers to agree to be included on the list. For example, create a link to an opt-in screen on your website or landing pages that offers a FREE newsletter or FREE product information when email details are provided.

To manage email lists, use a website such as *www.aweber.com*, *www.mailchimp.com* or similar that allows you to set schedules for email distribution and manage the content.

## 9.  Networking Events and Meetings

Networking is arguably the most effective form of marketing if you are in a service company or small company, because people like to work with people they know, or with whom they have a relationship.

The growth of breakfast clubs such as BNi is a testament to the popularity of this sort of event.

Getting the most out of Networking is just about knowing your product or service and being able to talk to people about it – make sure you take plenty of business cards with you.

The real key is turning up again and again until people get to know you and your business. Don't expect instant results, but you will get them eventually.

### 10. Joint Ventures

What I mean by joint ventures is collaborating with a non-competing third party to make use of their existing customers. Send direct mail, or an email about your service to someone else's customer database, and let them do the same with your customer database.

- Make sure you trust that the product or service the third party offer will be appreciated by your customers (and that they will do a good job) and that their customer base is the type that you want too.

- This leverages the pre-existing relationship that the other party has with their customers to your mutual advantage.

So there you have it, 10 activities to generate leads for your business. Try each of these, measure the response and then hone in on what works.

## The Sales System

As we have seen, sales is the act of taking a lead and turning into to a sale.

Before you even begin to sell, you should write out your sales system; this would obviously be different for every business type. If you haven't read *Chapter 3 'Organise Your Systems'*, then do this now.

Mapping out how the sales process works for you, will give you a better idea of how to organise sales to suit your own circumstances.

A system for doing anything in your business is a good idea. It stops repeated mistakes, helps you tailor a process and get the most from it. It helps a business find the best working practice and prevents it from repeating costly errors. A sales system is no exception. An effective sales system doesn't have to be a complicated one, but it should be made up of distinct steps.

## The process

The first thing to do is identify the steps in the sales process. For example:

- Enquiry.
- Meeting.
- Quote.
- Follow up.
- Close.

This is a simple outline of a process, but this can be expanded to explain what is said and done at each stage of the process, for example:

### Enquiry

✓ Take enquiry.

✓ Explain who we are.

✓ Send information.

## Meeting

- ✓ Gather key information.
- ✓ Complete form.

## Quote

- ✓ Take details.
- ✓ Price job.
- ✓ Send estimate with letter.

## Follow up

- ✓ Plan call.
- ✓ Make call.
- ✓ Reschedule call or allocate to lost job.

## Close

- ✓ Get agreement signed.
- ✓ Pass to delivery team.

Once you have done this for all stages, you can build up a picture of the sales process and start optimising it.

All sales start with an enquiry; these are either cold enquiries produced by your marketing, or are self-generated by prospecting that you have undertaken.

## Prospecting

Prospecting is the digging out of leads by networking, telemarketing or web research. Tools such as www.Linkedin.com can be useful for prospecting.

A useful tool, to optimise this aspect of your sales approach, is the categorisation of leads or potential customers. This is important because it can help you to identify what your response should be to each customer.

*For example, categories could include:*

- ➲ Potentials – anyone who could use your service.

- ➲ Suspects – any of the potentials likely to need your products.

- ➲ Leads – a suspect for whom we have contact details, who may have shown an interest, broken down into:

  - Cold Lead – someone who has a need for products, we have their name, but they don't know us.

  - Warm Lead – someone who needs our products, we have spoken to them, and they have shown some interest.

  - Hot Leads – someone who has expressed positive interest, we have spoken to them and started a relationship.

- ➲ Prospects – someone we have spoken to and discussed a specific piece of business.

- ➲ Qualified Prospect – someone who has a definite need, we have estimated, and within budget they have shown a potential to purchase.

- ➲ Quoted Prospects – someone who has almost committed to buy.

By analysing this process to this degree, you can encourage potentials through each stage and respond accordingly.

## Incoming enquiries

Whether the lead is generated from marketing or prospecting, you have to deal with incoming enquiries in the same optimised way to maximise your chances of converting it.

An enquiry is like a newly sprouted sapling; it needs nurturing and care to convert it into a sale. Treat it in the wrong way, and it will wither and die.

The questions you are asking at this point will have an effect on the ultimate outcome of the sale and will also help to decide if your time is being wasted.

Good practice is to have an enquiry form that is used by those taking the enquiry so that key information is collected with a uniform approach.

At this point, it is also worth trying to find out who the decision maker is, and what the budget for the product or service is.

**TOP TIP:** *Recording of telephone calls*

If you do get to the point of hiring a sales team, or someone to receive enquiry calls, then the best tool you can use for training and improvement purposes is to *record* the call. You can then use these recordings to guide the individual through what they said, what could have been said and how to improve the call.

**Do they qualify?**

Don't forget you are also checking if the customer qualifies to be a customer of yours. We have all had nightmare customers right? If you can learn to spot and qualify these nightmare customers at the initial enquiry stage, then you will save yourself time and headaches, although this isn't always possible you just need to be careful.

## The sales meeting

If you have a product or service that requires a sales meeting, then you are fortunate in the sense that you have an opportunity to influence your purchaser directly. If you sell remotely, this is much harder.

*The classic marketing model, AIDA, can easily be applied to the sales meeting:*

✓ Attention – getting the prospect to look at your offer.

✓   Interest – exciting their interest in the proposal.

✓   Desire – creating a wish to purchase.

✓   Action – moving them to buy.

## Preparation

If you have a sales meeting booked, make sure you have a copy of the initial enquiry form, and if possible, a record of the phone call that was made.

It is good practice to have a form or checklist for the sales meeting, and use it as a tool within the meeting.

This checklist can have a list of questions or details to gather, and acts as a reminder to you to ask all the relevant questions. It also gives the customer the impression that you are well organised – which of course you will be if you apply the instructions outlined in this book.

Make sure you know who you are meeting and where. Try not to be late, and think about what you are going to wear and drive.

Selling is often a perception exercise. If, during the course of the sales process, you have to undertake a visit to your potential customer's home, and you turn up looking scruffy, then the customer will judge you on that first impression. You may be able to turn them around with your sales patter, but you will have lost some credibility.

If you are visiting a house with a view to selling the customer a new bathroom, for example, and you turn up driving a Porsche, the perception will be that your prices are going to be too high. So think carefully about how you will be perceived, on every aspect of the contact with the customer.

*Real Life Example*

I once attended a sales meeting with a client who was looking for a consultant who could come in and train his sales team for his multi-million pound business. He interviewed various candidates, all purporting to be sales management consultants. After every meeting, he went to the window to look at the car being driven by the consultant.

Rightly or wrongly, this client of mine judged the candidates for the type of car they drove.

One consultant, for example, was driving a 10-year old people carrier that had, I must admit, seen better days. He didn't get the job.

This might not have been the best judgement of the potential consultant's ability to do the work, but a lot of people use the way you look, the car you drive, and the way you come across as criteria for buying from you.

## During the meeting

*If you can include the points from the list below in every sales meeting, making a sale will be easy.*

- ✓ **Find common ground** with the potential customer and start building a relationship with them.
- ✓ **Ask questions**, and gather information but do not sell.
- ✓ **State who you are, and reveal your USP** (unique selling point).
- ✓ **Match the offer** to what is being learned – the main pitch.

- ✓ **Double check the offer meets the customer's needs.**
- ✓ **Close the sale.**

## Find common ground

In 90% of sales meetings, the customer has a need for your product/service otherwise you wouldn't be there. They are motivated to come to the meeting or book the demonstration because they want to solve this need.

It is also a truism that people prefer to buy from people they know, so the first part of this process is to relate to the customer and find common ground.

In my accountancy business this is easy, because small business owners love to talk about their businesses almost as much as I love to hear about them. My background also helps, as I have worked in and around small business for so long, I can relate to their hopes, dreams and problems.

Most people can find common ground to talk about with their potential customers, and if you can then the sale will be so much easier. If not then it's going to be an uphill struggle.

Put yourself in the customer's shoes; ask questions to get information but do not sell yet.

## Ask questions

This stage may be mixed with the 'finding common ground' process as it can help you find common ground.

In her amazing book, '*The 7 Powers of Questions: Secrets to successful communication in life and at work*', Dorothy Leeds explains how questions are a powerful, yet simple means to finding specific or necessary information, establishing strong relationships and persuading and motivating others.

It's worth reviewing the questions you ask regularly, and also trying out new questions, to see if the response they elicit is any better.

In the questions stage, you will uncover the key issues that need to be solved, and if there are any objections that need to be resolved.

For example, a question I always ask is, *"What problems do you face in the business?"* This question is great because it demonstrates that I care about the issues my customer faces; it uncovers the real issues I need to resolve, and any other issues that I need to be aware of.

If a question fails to draw the correct answer, make a note and do not use it again, then try another. The sales meeting is a continuous improvement process, it can always be done better.

Find the correct set of questions that suit your product or service that help find out the issues that your customers have.

I often think I know the answers to the questions before I ask, but just the same, I always ask. Sometimes, I am surprised by an answer, but I use the questions stage as a diagnosis of the issues my customer is facing.

Whenever I buy a large ticket item like a new TV or carpet for the house, I always judge the salesperson. You can easily spot the good ones, but there are also many who appear disinterested because they don't ask questions.

By asking questions and finding out what the issue is you are more likely to sell a product or service that meets an actual need.

## State who you are and reveal your USP

Once you have asked your questions, which will be between 5 - 15 questions depending on the product/service you provide, explain who you are, what your ethos is, and what you aim to do. If you have done this right, these points should meet many of the issues the customer faces before you get started.

This stage is about establishing your credentials, and ensuring that the customer cannot object to you based on your qualification to sell. If, for example, you are the nation's leading canopy company, and have already installed into half the schools in the country, then now is the time to drop this into the conversation.

An issue often raised by prospective clients at the questions stage in sales meetings for my accountancy practice, is the one of having previously received unexpected invoices from their accountant. It's here that I let them know that we offer fixed fees, with a guarantee of no unexpected invoices. I also let them know that we will communicate with them regularly. These are my USP's and I know they resolve issues for the customer, although I do not directly refer to their issue at this stage, this comes next.

### Match the offer to what is being learned – main pitch

Now is the time to discuss the results of what you have learned and the language I use in this is:

- ✓ *"So you mentioned you could never get good financial information, well our service provides this by..."*

- ✓ *"You mentioned that you never knew what your invoice would be, well..."*

- ✓ *"You said your previous accountant was not proactive enough, well we have systems in place to ensure..."*

This may seem a little blatant because it is exactly what the customer wants to know, but it also happens to be truthful. I would never advocate telling them things that aren't true; in my case I have tailored my service to meet the needs of my customer, so it's easy.

It should be easy for you to do this as well. If the sale is right for the customer, it's your job to point out why this is so. If the sale is wrong for the customer, you shouldn't push it because mis-selling will lead to unhappy customers and problems in the future, and you should walk away after explaining your reasons.

You should have, by the end of this process, explained your service, and how it meets every one of the customer's needs.

## Double check the offer meets the customer's needs

Now is the time to re-iterate and check that what you are offering meets the needs. You can even ask another powerful question: *"Has what we discussed helped meet your needs?"*

Now would be a good point to step back and let the customer talk more. If you don't stop talking, then you cannot hear their objections, or their willingness to order.

None of this process is about the hard sell; it's all about demonstrating how your product or service meets your customer's needs. If you believe in what you are selling, you owe it to your customer to demonstrate it in the best light.

## Close the Sale

*Closing the sale is the final act of getting the signature on the order.*

I never force the close, what's the point? I think a close should be a natural conclusion to the above.

For a long time, I was under the impression that my new customers could not be closed in the meeting, but I was wrong. It turned out that it was down to me being uncomfortable with asking for the order, and not having that ability to ask the customer to sign for the order prevented the close – I was getting in my own way.

I have learned to remain silent while the customer reads the order form and makes their decision. If they want more time to think, then I explain how they can place their order later on, if they want to make the decision there and then, I explain what we need to do. I give them the opportunity to sign up there and then, but I do not force this. I no longer get in my own way. If I have completed steps 1 – 5 correctly, the close comes naturally. If the customer isn't ready, then I leave the paperwork with them and follow up later.

### Real Life Example

A few examples ago we met Harry, a supplier of high-end kitchens. When I first met him, he explained to me that his customers were hard to close; he had to do many drawings and revisions before getting them to sign.

He told me of one situation where a potential customer of his had asked for one final revision before placing the order, which appeared to be a buying signal (a customer indicating that they were ready to buy). Harry made the revision, but his potential customer never signed. Something happened between this buying signal and the order.

At that point, Harry should have said, "I am happy to make the revision subject to a signed order". His potential customer wanted the product; they were happy with the countless revisions he had made, and needed just one more. I bet if he had asked them, they would have signed the order, Harry would have made the revision, and the job would have gone ahead. If he had asked at that point, at least he would have known what the outcome would be, because I think if they hadn't signed the order then, they wouldn't be likely to at any point, and ultimately they didn't.

## After the meeting

After the meeting, make sure the order is processed quickly and efficiently, and the customer is kept in the loop of its progress

If you have been unable to close in the meeting, and the customer requires a quote, then produce this quickly and always, without fail, follow up the quote.

## To summarise:

Recognise that there is a *difference* between **sales** and **marketing**. Broadly speaking, marketing is to generate the lead and sales is to close it.

*Before you begin any lead-generating activity ask yourself four key questions:*

1. Who are you trying to reach?

2. What action do you want them to take when you reach them?

3. How much are you willing to spend on each new lead?

4. How are you going to measure this activity to see that it's effective?

To organise your approach, use a *spreadsheet* to plan all your marketing activities. If it helps, use a calendar to set out scheduled activities.

Don't spend lots of money on any one activity; test different approaches, measure the response, and then increase spend on the ones that work.

The key to good sales is having a *good system*. Write one down, then test and refine it. If you use others to make your sales, create a sales system for them and ensure they follow it. If you include a sales meeting in your sales system, detail how you want this meeting to pan out.

*Don't forget to try and structure the meeting to include these elements:*

- ✓ **Find common ground** with the potential customer and start building a relationship with them.
- ✓ **Ask questions**, and gather information but do not sell.
- ✓ **State who you are, and reveal your USP** (unique selling point).
- ✓ **Match the offer** to what is being learned – the main pitch.
- ✓ Double check the **offer meets the customer's needs**.
- ✓ **Close the sale.**

# Chapter 6: Organise Your Numbers

*"If you don't drive your business, you will be
driven out of business."*
**B.C. Forbes**

The majority of this book is about how to make your business scalable and more profitable by getting organised. This chapter is slightly different, in that it is about understanding your numbers.

Do you often feel that your accountant speaks a different language, or that they have more knowledge of your business's performance than you do? The reason is, because they hold the knowledge that is described in this chapter.

The finances of the business are fundamental; they are the main reason we do business, so it's important to take control of them.

Your business has a much higher chance of failure if you do not understand how the finances work, or alternatively, your business has a much greater chance of success if you do understand the numbers. Even a few pieces of information, such as how much you need to sell each month to make a profit can make all the difference.

You don't need to be a mathematician to understand your business's finances, but you do need to make an effort to get your head around some of the basics.

## The Tale of Two Brothers

**John** has good control over the cash in the business; he knows who owes him money and what he has in the bank.

What he doesn't understand is the profit of the business.

John's accountant produced his accounts each year, but the profit didn't seem to correspond with the cash in the bank. In fact, often his profit seemed okay, but his cash was low. Even after his accountant explained it to him, he still couldn't get his head around it.

Cash was always tight, and he never actually knew if he had enough to cover the next month's costs.

Because he didn't know his profitability, it meant that he didn't know what his profitable work was, what his profitable months were, and where he was losing money. Profit didn't drive strategy; it was always a gut feeling, and this worked okay, but it didn't maximise profit.

John has never been able to understand the key performance indicators in his business. He wouldn't know where to start.

Stephen decided early on, to become an expert, or at least a well-informed amateur. He realised that if he knew the difference between the Profit and Loss and the Balance Sheet, he could have meaningful conversations with his accountant, and would be in control of his business.

Stephen bought an audio book, used the Internet to read around the subject, and did some training. Slowly but surely, he built up a reasonable knowledge. Once he became confident, he asked his accountant to make sure he got the management accounts on a monthly basis. He used these, along with budgets, as a basis for a monthly finance meeting. At first he invited his accountant to these, and in time he took over.

This meeting reviewed the business's monthly performance and key performance indicators, and became the control for the business.

Stephen completed a short-term cash forecast each week, so that he knew he had enough cash to cover everything. Sometimes the forecast showed he didn't have enough, but he knew in advance, and was able to do something about it.

The numbers in Stephen's business led the strategy of the business, and with this he was able to maximise profit.

## Bookkeeping Software

Before attempting to get a proper understanding of your finances, or scale your business, you will need a proper bookkeeping package, not just a simple spreadsheet.

*Most bookkeeping packages include:*

1.  **A Profit and Loss report.**

2.  **A Balance Sheet.**

3.  **A list of debtors – customer who owe you money.**

4.  **A list of creditors – suppliers you owe money to.**

5.  **The ability to post adjustments.**

We recommend *www.xero.com* because it gives you all the benefits of the above, and is cloud-based, meaning that you can collaborate remotely with your bookkeeper, your accountant, and anyone else you want included.

## Understand <u>Your</u> Accounts

The old maxim goes, *"Turnover is vanity, profit is sanity and cash is reality."* If you focus solely on any one of these, then you won't be in full control of your business.

Most small businesses hire a bookkeeper to ensure the VAT is done correctly. Bookkeepers generally process the source information – receipts, invoices and bank statements etc., and shouldn't be confused with accountants, who convert the books into year-end accounts, and ensure that you do not pay too much or too little tax.

When businesses owners don't have the time for bookkeeping, then hiring a bookkeeper can be a good idea. However, knowledge is power, and if you don't understand what your bookkeeper is doing, then they will have the power, not you.

Most bookkeepers do a good job, but if you do not understand the underlying principles of your figures, then you are as about knowledgeable as the person who doesn't know about anything about their car on a trip to the garage. They may not get ripped off, but would they know if they were?

The next part of this chapter is split into two parts. The first is the fundamental information that, in my opinion, you ought to know to even be in business, and the second is about information you should aim to be aware of.

## Part 1: The Basics

Here are some basic principles you need to know and understand, and I apologise if this is a bit simplistic, but it's designed for those with no knowledge of the subject at all.

### *The two fundamental reports in your business:*

1.  **Profit and Loss.**
2.  **Balance Sheet.**

*These two reports explained:*

## Profit and Loss

This shows the sales or turnover of the business, and the expenses or costs. Once you subtract all the expenses from the sales, you get the net profit. The Profit and Loss can be calculated daily, weekly, monthly or by department.

If you want to know how profitable your business is you use this report. Profit is a big part of what drives most businesses, so this report is essential.

The Profit of your business is calculated on this report, it lists:

- ➲ Sales – the invoiced sales or turnover of the business.
- ➲ Cost of Sales – the costs associated with the sales you have made (also called variable costs).
- ➲ Gross Profit – sales less cost of sales.
- ➲ Overheads – the costs associated with your business (rent, heat, etc.) also called fixed costs.
- ➲ Net Profit – gross profit less overheads.

The Profit and Loss is a one-period statement, either one month, one quarter, one year etc.

**Some key ratios found in the Profit and Loss are:**

Gross Profit % = Gross Profit / Sales x 100

Net Profit % = Net Profit / Sales x 100

## Balance Sheet

The Balance Sheet is a summary of the assets, what the business is owed or owns, and liabilities, what the business owes. It shows what would be left if the business ceased, if all assets were sold, and all liabilities were paid off. The Balance

Sheet is a rolling figure and is always made up to a date (up to the end of the month, or year for example).

This is balanced against your profits and your owner's interest, i.e. share capital.

The Balance Sheet is continuous, but is viewed by taking a snapshot at any point in time, e.g. at the end of the financial year.

*The headings on the Balance Sheet are:*

- ➲ Fixed Assets (see below).
- ➲ Current Assets = stock, trade debtors, bank and cash.
- ➲ Current Liabilities = trade creditors.
- ➲ Long Term Liabilities = loans.
- ➲ Net Assets = fixed assets and current assets less all liabilities.
- ➲ Retained Profit = previous year's profit.
- ➲ Profit for Year = this year's profit.
- ➲ Share Capital and Reserves.

**Why is it called a Balance Sheet?**

A Balance Sheet is so called because it has two halves that must always balance. In other words the top half of the Balance Sheet must always balance with the bottom half of the Balance Sheet.

The reason the two halves balance is to act as a check for bookkeeping entries, and the way it is balanced is because of double entry bookkeeping. *See Part 2* (page 135) for an insight into how double entry bookkeeping works.

If you still don't understand quite what a Balance Sheet is, or how this is relevant, then I can recommend 'Accounts Demystified' by Anthony Rice. The author goes into much more depth about this subject and it's quite an excellent book.

## Some other accounting terminology explained

### Cash is king, but it is not profit

Your bank balance is not your profitability, and it cannot show you how well you are doing on a monthly basis. Do not assume that you have made a profit just because you have cash.

As a broad rule, cash in the bank is a good indicator, but it cannot help you pinpoint your successes, or where you are not doing well. See *'Accurate Management Accounts'* in part 2 for how to achieve this.

### Gross Profit

Gross Profit is calculated as:

*Sales, less cost of sales*

Cost of sales (or the costs associated with the sales you have made) is:

*Opening stock, plus purchases, less closing stock, and this is deducted from sales to get your Gross profit.*

So in a month, if you made sales of £1,000 and purchases of £600, your gross profit would be £400.

To calculate Gross Profit % (GP%), Gross Profit is divided by sales.

So £400 / £1,000 x 100 = 40%

Only direct costs should be included in purchases (cost of sales) i.e., only costs that you incur because you have made a sale.

The direct costs for a plumber are for the parts he uses, any subcontractors, but not his apprentice as he is paid whatever work is done, or his telephone bill.

## Break-even

Break-even turnover is the amount of sales that makes your profit equal zero.

Each sale makes a contribution to the overheads.

So a sale of £1,000 with costs of £600 will have a £400 gross profit, and that's £400 towards overheads.

The easiest way to calculate break-even turnover, is to divide your GP% by your overheads.

Let's assume you have an overhead (fixed costs) of £100,000 per annum, and a GP% of 40%. We divide £100,000 by 40% or .4; this will give a break-even turnover of £250,000. So you will need to sell £250,000 per annum at 40% to get a Gross profit of £100,000 to break-even and cover your overheads. In other words you need to sell £250,000 of product or service to make no profit at all.

Divide the break-even sales by 12 and you get a break-even monthly sales target of £20,833. This is the amount of sales you need to make each month to make £0 profit.

## Debtors or Receivables

Debtors owe the business money, their debts (receivables)can be can split into Trade Debts (amounts owed by customers) and other debtors (other amounts owed to the business).

Trade Debtors should be presented in a chronologically ordered report, starting with the oldest, so that you can chase them in date order. This is known as an aged debtors report.

## Creditors or Payables

Creditors are owed money by the business, and these payables can be split between Trade Creditors (amounts owed to suppliers) and other creditors (such as loans).

Trade Creditors should also be presented in a chronologically ordered report, starting with the oldest, so you pay only the oldest first.

In the year-end accounts produced by your accountant, creditors are split between short and long term. Short term is less than one year and long term over a year.

## Stock

Stock is anything you have bought to sell, or use directly that still remains at the end of a period. For example, if you bought two widgets, sold one and had one left, the remaining one is closing stock.

As mentioned earlier, stock makes up part of the all-important Gross Profit calculation. Opening stock is added to purchases, and closing stock is deducted to arrive at the cost of your sales. Stock is discussed in more detail in the *'Getting accurate management accounts'* in part 2.

## Overheads, Cost of Sales or Fixed Assets

A cost to your business can be categorised either as an overhead (a fixed cost), a cost of sale (a variable cost) or a fixed asset. But how do you decide where each item should go?

The first question to ask is if the cost qualifies as a fixed asset? A fixed asset is a cost that will last more than a year.

If it is a fixed asset the item will be recognised in the Balance Sheet and won't immediately show in the Profit and Loss.

If you have decided the cost is not a fixed asset then it's either a cost of sale or an overhead.

A cost of sale is something that is directly attributable to the sales you make and an overhead would probably happen if you made no sales at all.

For example, a plumber buys a jet machine to clear drains, and the chemicals to use in it. The jet machine will last for five years, and the chemicals for five weeks. The chemicals are a cost of sale and the jet machine is a fixed asset. I explain below why it's important to classify costs correctly in more detail in *Part 2*.

## Fixed Assets

Fixed assets are held on the Balance Sheet and their costs are released to the Profit and Loss over their useful life, e.g. five years, in the form of depreciation. Depreciation is the cost of the fixed asset being taken into the Profit and Loss as an overhead. If the useful life is five years then the amount of depreciation taken to the Profit and Loss each year will 1/5 of the cost of the item.

When a cost isn't a fixed asset, it is charged to the Profit and Loss in the period it is incurred.

The point of depreciation is to accurately reflect the cost of the fixed asset by taking a proportion of it back into the Profit and Loss for each accounting period.

Now you may be thinking what happens if I pay for something that will last five weeks, one week before the year end? This is known as a prepayment, and technically should be excluded from your accounts at the year-end. We will go into more detail in the *'Getting accurate management accounts'* in *Part 2*.

*Phew!*

That is a lot of information in a short time, but this is the terminology you will need to get familiar with when you're running your business.

If you spend time getting to know your accounts, you will be in a much better position to evaluate the performance of your business, and you will reduce your reliance on your bookkeeper and accountant. You can then request that your bookkeeper produces monthly reports that you can use to spot any potential problems in your business.

*If they have all the knowledge, you will never be in complete control of the business.*

At this point, you may want to read this section again until it makes sense to you. When you are ready, read on...

# Part 2 - Accounts in More Detail

We are going to delve a bit deeper now and look at accounts in more detail! *If you want to skip this bit, head to page 150 and get stuck in on Pricing*

### *The basics of double entry bookkeeping*

If you want to get a proper understanding of your numbers, it is useful to have some background knowledge of the method used to create them.

Don't worry, this won't be too taxing and it may just click with you, so it's worth a try.

Double entry is so called because every entry in the books has two effects.

A debit is shown as **DR** (Debit Remittance), and a credit shown as **CR** (Credit Remittance).

Every **debit** and **credit** will either affect the *Profit and Loss*, the *Balance Sheet* or both.

So, for example, when a sale is made for cash for say £100– the DR (Debit) goes to Bank, to represent the cash received, and the CR (Credit) goes to Sales.

*Visually it might look like this:*

|  | DR | CR |
|---|---|---|
| DR Bank | £100 | |
| CR Sales | | £100 |

When a sale is made for credit, the **DR** goes to **Debtors**, and the **CR** goes to **Sales**.

|  | DR | CR |
|---|---|---|
| DR Debtors | £100 | |
| CR Sales | | £100 |

These tables above are examples of an entry that affects both the *Profit and Loss* and the *Balance Sheet.*

When a fixed asset is purchased for cash, e.g. a new van costing £10,000, a **DR** goes to *Fixed Assets* and a **CR** goes to *Bank* (money out).

*Visually it might look like this:*

|  | DR | CR |
|---|---|---|
| DR Fixed Asset | £10,000 | |
| CR Bank | | £10,000 |

When a van is bought for credit a **DR** goes to **Fixed Assets**, but the **CR** goes to **Creditors** (you owe this money).

*Visually it might look like this:*

|  | DR | CR |
|---|---|---|
| **DR Fixed Asset** | £10,000 | |
| **CR Creditors** | | £10,000 |

These tables above are examples of an entry that affects *Balance Sheet*.

So why does it balance?

You can see on all the entries above the total of the **DR** Column and the total of the **CR** column is the same. *Each **DR** has a Corresponding **CR**.*

That's fine for only Balance Sheet entries, as each **DR** and **CR** only affect the Balance Sheet. But what about when the **DR** is in the *Profit and Loss* and the **CR** is in the *Balance Sheet* (as in a sale made for cash)

|  | DR | CR |
|---|---|---|
| **DR Bank (Balance Sheet)** | £100 | |
| **CR Sales (Profit and Loss)** | | £100 |

The balance occurs because the *Profit and Loss* nets off to one figure, the net profit, and this is entered on the balancing side of the Balance Sheet.

This means that the entries you made in *Profit and Loss* will appear on the *Balance Sheet* eventually, and match or balance the entries you made on the Balance Sheet in the first place.

**Example**

Let's look at *five transactions* for my new business selling widgets, and follow them through to the *Profit and Loss* and *Balance Sheet*.

1. I put £10,000 into the business bank account personally.

2. I buy goods worth £5,000 from the bank account.

3. I sell goods for cash for £7,500.

4. I sell goods worth £2,000 on credit.

5. I pay rent for £1,000 from the business bank account.

*The double entry for these items would be:*

|  |  | DR | CR |
|---|---|---|---|
| 1. | DR Bank | £10,000 | |
| | CR Directors Loan Accounts | | £10,000 |
| 2. | DR Purchases | £5,000 | |
| | CR Bank Accounts | | £5,000 |
| 3. | DR Bank | £7,500 | |
| | CR Sales | | £7,500 |
| 4. | DR Debtors | £2,000 | |
| | CR Sales | | £2,000 |
| 5. | DR Rent | £1,000 | |
| | CR Bank | | £1,000 |

*The Trial Balance for the above will look like this:*

|  | DR | CR |
|---|---|---|
| Sales | | £9,500 |
| Purchases | £5,000 | |
| Rent | £1,000 | |
| Bank | £11,500 | |
| Debtors | £2,000 | |
| Directors Loan | | £10,000 |
| Total | £19,500 | £19,500 |

*The Profit and Loss for the above will look like this:*

|  | DR | CR |
|---|---|---|
| Sales | | £9,500 |
| Purchases | £5,000 | |
| Gross Profit | | £4,500 |
| Rent | £1,000 | |
| Net Profit | | £3,500 |

*The Balance Sheet will look like this:*

|  | DR | CR |
|---|---|---|
| Bank | £11,500 | |
| Debtors | £2,000 | |
| Directors Loan | | £10,000 |
| Net Assets | | £3,500 |
| Profit and Loss | | £3,500 |

You can see that the Profit and Loss has netted off to one figure, the Net Profit of £3,500, and this is the figure that makes the Balance Sheet balance. The top half of the Balance Sheet contains the Bank, Debtors and Directors Loan and equals £3,500 when netted off, and the bottom half contains the £3,500 profit from the Profit and Loss.

If you want to find out more, there are whole books dedicated to the subject. However I don't think, as a business owner, you need to fully understand double entry bookkeeping to get an understanding of your accounts, but it does help to have an idea of how it works.

## Trial Balance

As we have seen, the Trial Balance is a *summary of all the balances* in your accounts, separating them out as either:

- Debits - Assets and Expenses.
- Credits - Income or Liabilities.

The Trial Balance, as the name suggest, should balance. On computerised accounts packages, if it doesn't, a suspense account will be created to make it balance.

The Trial Balance is used by your accountant, to produce your statutory financial statements. It's also useful for you as an overview of the balances in your accounts.

## Accurate Management Accounts

Management accounts are simply Profit and Loss reports, and to a lesser extent Balance Sheet reports, that are frequently produced for your business. Normally, when we talk about accounts, we think of the statutory accounts produced by your accountant once a year to keep the taxman happy. Management accounts aren't for anyone else, they are for you and should be produced regularly, either monthly or quarterly.

Next, I will look at why it's so important to have accurate management accounts, and why these should not be solely for larger companies. I'll examine why these are even more important to your business if cash is tight and profit is scarce.

The decisions you make for your business can mean the difference between your business surviving or failing, and these need to be made on the back of good financial data.

Many businesses and business people judge how well they are doing by a healthy bank balance. Unfortunately, a *large amount of cash in your bank can hide a multitude of sins in your business.*

It is similar to the runner who smokes 20 cigarettes a day. He is fortunate that he can run a mile in 10 minutes, and complete a marathon in under four hours. He thinks that smoking has no effect on him as his times are good, but imagine what he could do if he didn't smoke!

Accurate management accounts will help you find out how well your business is really doing, what areas need improving, and which are making you your profit.

Most bookkeeping packages will produce a Profit and Loss at the click of a button, but for accuracy there are several adjustments that need to be made, and these are:

- ➲ **Stock.**
- ➲ **Pre-payments.**
- ➲ **Accruals.**
- ➲ **Depreciation.**
- ➲ **Wages.**

The first step is to get an accurate Gross Profit figure on a monthly basis. Do this by matching the sales you make in any one month, to the direct costs.

*For example:*

You sell 5 units at £1,000, but buy 7 at £500; your accounts show a Gross Profit £1,500.

- ➲ Sales = £5,000
- ➲ Costs = (£3,500)
- ➲ Profit = £1,500

*This looks good right?*

However, this isn't accurate as you kept *two units at £500* in stock, and didn't sell them until the following month.

**So your Gross Profit should be £2,500.**

- ✓ Sales = £5,000
- ✓ Costs = (£3,500)
- ✓ Stock = (£1,000)
- ✓ Profit = £2,500

*You have made £2,500 not £1,500.*

By carefully matching any sales to their direct costs, and removing any unsold items, you will show a *more accurate* Gross Profit.

This applies equally to other direct costs incurred in the month that relate to sales in future months, such as labour or material costs.

You can take this further by allocating each sale a reference, matching each cost by reference, and producing a Gross Profit by product. This will show you which products are giving you the best, and the worse Gross Profit.

## Stock

If your business is a stock-based business, then *your stock is the biggest influencer of an accurate Gross Profit.*

To measure stock, first give it a value at the end of the month, and remove this from your purchases to show you exactly what has been purchased in the month.

Sales minus purchases less stock will be your Gross Profit.

The next month, you should calculate the closing stock, but this time remove this from last month's closing stock, plus this month's purchases, to come up with this month's total purchases.

**SOFTWARE TIP:** To get an accurate stock level, you may want to employ a stock control system; you can find many of them online. Check out: *www.unleashedsoftware.com, www.tradegecko.co.uk* and *www.tidystock.co.uk*

## Overheads

Once your Gross Profit is correct, it's time to sort out the overheads. The most common method of recording overheads is on a cash basis. This means as we pay for it, we record it.

Now consider this example. In January, we pay rent for three months, rates for three months, and the telephone bill for the last quarter. Our accounts look like this:

<u>Gross Profit     £2,500</u>

- ➲ Rent          (£1,500)
- ➲ Rates         (£750)
- ➲ Telephone     (£250)

*Gross Profit less overheads equals:*

- ➲ Net Profit    **£0.00**

Now in consider what happens in February:

<u>Gross Profit     £2,500</u>

- ➲ Rent          £0
- ➲ Rates         £0
- ➲ Telephone     £0

*Gross Profit less overheads equals:*

- ➲ Net Profit    **£2,500**

All three of these *expenses* do not belong completely in January because rent and rates are for three months, and telephone is for the previous quarter.

*January should look like this:*

<u>Gross Profit   £2,500</u>

- ✓ Rent          £500
- ✓ Rates         £250
- ✓ Telephone   £83

*Gross Profit less overheads equals:*

- ✓ Profit          **£1,667**

*February should look like this:*

<u>Gross Profit   £2,500</u>

- ✓ Rent          £500
- ✓ Rates         £250
- ✓ Telephone   £83

*Gross Profit less overheads equals:*

- ✓ Profit          **£1,667**

If you made decisions based on how much profit you have made in each month, you could think that January was bad, and have a big sales push, and February was great, so you then ease back, but technically you're basing decisions on an incomplete picture.

**Accurate overheads**

To get your overheads correct in each month, you may need to move things about a bit. If you have paid something in advance (pre-paid) this may need to be moved to a later date, or spread out.

If you have incurred a cost, but not received the invoice yet, you may need to record the cost in your books in advance – this is called *posting an accrual.*

*To clarify:*

**Prepayments** –paying something in advance e.g. rates.

**Accruals** – accounting for an expense you are paying in arrears e.g. *telephone.*

The increased use of the monthly direct debit has eliminated much of the need to account for these items, but if you don't pay for something in the month you use it, then it's either a prepayment or you should have accrued for it.

## Pre-payments

A good example of a pre-payment is business rates, paid for a year in advance.

If you pay the rates in January, then January's net profit will be low, and the rest of the year will not be accurate. What you need to do is to split this invoice over the time period you incur the expense.

If you use a software package to do your bookkeeping, then post the invoice to a Balance Sheet code when you first get it. You can do this by using a supplier account, and pointing the code to the Balance Sheet, then you must journal this out, in this example, 1/12th every month to the Profit and Loss.

## Accruals

Accruals will take a bit more planning, because you're trying to predict the future, by estimating what expenses you should allocate to each month.

This is easier than predicting the future, because you have some history to use. For example, we know when we get the telephone bill it's usually roughly £300 a quarter. We therefore need to allocate £100 a month to pay it.

To do this on your accounting package, you will need to post a *journal*. A journal is an adjustment to bookkeeping that is made up of a **DR** and a **CR.**

*In this case we would post this journal each month for 3 months:*

|  | DR | CR |
|---|---|---|
| DR - Telephone | £100 | |
| CR - Accruals | | £100 |

At the end of the three months, the accrual account will have a balance of £300 on it, and when the bill comes in you will need to post this to the Accruals account as well. Invariably the actual bill won't be exactly £300, so any difference or balance left in the accruals account will need to be posted back to telephone expenses.

Now each month you will have at least accounted for some telephone costs even if it's not 100% accurate.

If your prediction is horribly wrong, and the bill is for a £1000, then you may wish to correct each of the three months. If it is £350, you may just want to put this through the last month.

The same applies for all overhead items that are paid in arrears.

## Depreciation

We know from earlier that fixed assets are costs that should be spread across, or taken to the Profit and Loss as an overhead over their useful lives. *The method of doing this is called depreciation.*

Therefore depreciation is just the *cost of the fixed asset spread over its lifetime.*

Depreciation is important for accurate management accounts, as by posting it, you are accurately reflecting the cost of these large ticket items in the Profit and Loss.

Fixed assets are one of the big reasons why your year-end accounts, prepared by your accountant, do not match your management accounts. For example, you may include all computer expenditure in your overheads, but your accountant will strip this out and charge depreciation instead.

Depreciation is not easy to calculate, as there are several method options. However, I have included a **Fixed Asset Register** on the website (see below) that accompanies this book.

If you can't be bothered to keep your own fixed asset register ask your accountant to give you a monthly depreciation journal for you to post. If you use *www.xero.com* your accountant can simply log on and do this for you.

Whatever you do, *don't include fixed assets in your overheads.* A good rule of thumb is anything that costs over £200 (that lasts more than a year) should be added to the register and depreciation journals should be posted.

 Visit **book.theorganisedbusiness.co.uk** to download your *'Fixed Asset Register'*

## Wages

Wages are another important area that can be incorrectly posted in the books. To be accurate you really need to post a wages journal. Again, your accountant can provide this for you to post.

Wages in the Profit and Loss need to show the total cost of your employees for the month in question, including the payroll taxes you are paying for them (PAYE and National Insurance), and not just the net wages (the amount you pay employees).

*If you are going to attempt this journal yourself it should look like this:*

|  | DR | CR |
|---|---|---|
| P&L Gross Wages | X | |
| P&L Employers NI | X | |
| B/S Net Wages | | X |
| B/S PAYE and NI | | X |

*When you pay the wages and post the bank payment to the Balance Sheet, the double entry for this payment will look like this:*

|  | DR | CR |
|---|---|---|
| B/S NET WAGES | X | |
| B/S Bank | | X |

If you can identify how to make these simple adjustments, you will then start to get accurate monthly figures. You will have now joined the minority of small, and probably medium businesses, in knowing exactly what your profit is each month. Now you are a step closer to knowing if you have a profitable business or not.

# Pricing

What you charge the customer has *huge implications* to the profitability of your business. Setting the price too low or too high could mean you will never make a profit.

Pricing is one of the most difficult aspects to get right, the price you set has to generate a profit, be set to a level that your customers actually want to pay and give off the right perception, in terms of quality, about your product or service.

Many businesses charge what the customer is willing to pay, without reviewing what it is doing to their profit. Pricing low to increase turnover is fine, if the *increase in turnover* covers the costs. Like many things in business and in life, it's a balance. Price it too high and no one will buy and you won't make a profit, price it too low and everyone will buy, but you won't make a profit.

Without getting too technical, this can be illustrated with this graph.

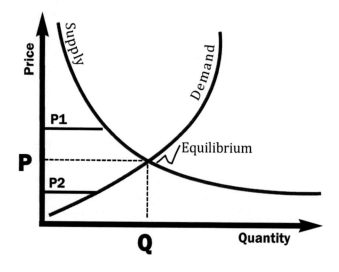

The price of a product is determined by a balance between supply at each price, and the desires of those with purchasing power at each price (demand). Price is at Equilibrium when the *Demand Curve* crosses the *Supply Curve*.

This optimal price will result in the quantity of goods sold – Q. If you look at the point **P1** you will see that when the price is *too high demand drops* off, and you have too much supply, and conversely at **P2** when the price is *too low, demand is too high* for the supply, and you have shortages.

## So how do you price?

There are many methods of pricing, but as a general rule I would always *calculate what your costs are*. You need to know what it costs you, directly and indirectly, to supply the product or service. If you know this, you can then add to the costs to ensure you make a profit.

The amount you add to the costs will be determined by the market, the competition, your relationship with the customer, if you have a monopoly on the product, and in some cases what you can get away with.

---

### Real Life Example

About a year ago I met with a client who was running a small business that was failing. She employed me on a mini turnaround session, called *'Getting Your Business Back on Track'*, where I go into a small business four times in one month, and we intensely review what is going wrong. At the end of that time, the business will either be cured, or we will have identified that the business can't work.

On day one, we talk through everything without looking for solutions, and then we go to work. This particular lady, called Sarah, was running an electrical services company with her husband Tom. I asked them how they priced their services, and she said, *"We charge £50 per socket, £30 per metre etc."* I asked how they had arrived at these prices and she said, *"It's the way Tom did it at the last place he worked."*

The next question I asked was, *"Do you track Profit and Loss on a job-by-job basis?"* Of course, she answered no. So I set her two exercises; the first to review a job in the last six weeks, and tell me if she had achieved a profit or loss, and secondly to look at all their prices to review their basis, and figure out what the costs were on these.

When we next sat down, she looked tired and worried, and it turned out that not only had she made a loss on the job she had reviewed, she had pretty much made a loss on all the completed jobs in the previous six weeks. On top of that, she had reviewed the set prices, and they were lower than the costs.

Armed with this knowledge, we designed a simple pricing sheet (available as a download) that takes in all the costs of a job, which you then multiply by a number of your choice to get to a price.

Using this sheet, it showed she needed to price 20% higher than she had previously, which was worrying for her, but crucially these prices meant she would make a profit.

So she priced under the new regime, and not one of her regular customers mentioned the price increase.

We went on to implement many of the items in this book and made some real improvements in the business.

## *Value pricing*

**A word of warning** - pricing based only on cost could rob you of potential profit, because cost-based pricing does not take into account a huge factor – which is the *'What is the customer willing to pay for it?'* factor.

Many customers are happy to pay a premium for a service, if they perceive they are getting more value from it, or that the product gives them some immeasurable benefit, like the kudos of owning it. For example, people are willing to pay more for an iPhone than other smart phones because of the brand image. If you price on cost only, you could lose this premium aspect. This is one reason why pricing is so difficult.

Now is a good time to review your prices and your costs, and see if the services or products you supply are priced correctly.

It is worth testing the price by raising it, and measuring the customer response a few times to find your equilibrium price.

# Key Performance Indicators – KPIs

I mentioned KPIs in *Chapter 1*, and if you're *unfamiliar with them, then please read on!*

The abbreviation KPI is jargon, but in full, explains the concept beautifully. KPIs are the **Key Indicators in your business that guarantee the Performance of it.** These can be any metric you choose, but they are set so that if you meet them, it will guarantee success.

KPIs allow you to monitor the performance of your business, and to spot when something is going wrong and quickly adjust it. They give you the control over the business and allow you to be in the driving seat.

The simplest KPI and the easiest to measure is sales turnover.

*Using turnover as a basis, ask yourself:*

**What is the level of turnover you need to reach in order to make a profit?**

*Once you have this you can then ask:*

**How many units of your product, man-hours, or personal hours do you need to sell to meet this level of turnover?**

**How many sales enquiries do you need to convert to achieve this level of sales?**

Once you have identified the *KPIs* in your business, you need to go about measuring and tracking them to see if they are achieved or not. Once you do this, you will start to look at your business in a different light.

The first step in identifying your *Key Performance Indicators* is to think about the information that you really want to know in a specific time period.

**Do you want to know each week...**

- The number of sales enquiries?
- The number of sales closed?
- The value of sales closed?
- The number of sales lost?
- The cash in the bank?
- The level of bad debt?
- The number of products sold?
- The number of products returned?
- The number of times sales representatives were late?
- The number of days staff missed?
- The number of quotes produced?
- The number of follow up calls made?

- The number of visitors to the shop?
- The number of visitors to the website?
- The average order value of each customer?
- The average value of each job lost?
- The number of sales from existing customers?
- The marketing spend on new customers?
- The number of sales from existing customers?
- The marketing spend on existing customers?

There is no end to the list in your business, but the trick is identifying the key information you need as an owner, so that you can use it as the barometer of your businesses performance.

Once you have identified these, you need to figure out a way to measure your KPIs regularly. I would create a spreadsheet to plot these in weekly, so you can track them over time, then the numbers will become truly useful.

## To summarise:

This was another heavy chapter, but hopefully you can see the importance of finances.

Many small business shy away from their finances, and this is one of the reasons *so many businesses fail.* The financial reality of the business should be assessed, reviewed and dealt with. **Knowledge is power, so the small business owner who understands his finances will win out in the end.**

*Here is what we have covered:*

- There are two fundamental reports in your business – the *Profit and Loss* and the *Balance Sheet*. The Profit and Loss gives you the profit of the business and is for a set period, month, quarter or year.

- The Balance Sheets gives you, your businesses net asset value, shows everything you owe and are owed, and is made up to a certain date. It's cumulative so it runs from day one in your business up to the date you are reviewing.

- Your bank balance is not your profitability, and it cannot show you how well you are doing on a monthly basis. Do not assume that you have profit just because you have cash.

- Gross Profit is calculated as sales, less cost of sales

  To calculate Gross Profit % (GP%), Gross Profit is divided by sales and then multiplied by 100.

- Break-even Turnover is the point of sales that your profit equals zero. The easiest way to calculate your break-even turnover, is to divide your overheads by your GP%.

- Debtors or Receivables are amounts owed to the buisness.

- Creditors or Payables are the amounts the business owes.

- Stock is anything you have bought to sell, or use directly that still remains at the end of a period.

- A cost to your business can be categorised either as an overhead (a fixed cost), a cost of sale (a variable costs) or a fixed asset.

- Fixed Assets are held on the Balance Sheet and then released over their useful life, e.g. five years in the form of depreciation.

To truly get meaning from your accounts you need to get accurate management accounts. To do this you will need to at least make adjustments for:

- ➲ Stock.
- ➲ Pre-payments.
- ➲ Accruals.
- ➲ Depreciation.
- ➲ Wages.

It's important to make sure your pricing is accurate, and a good place to start is making sure it at least covers your costs, but don't forget the customer may be willing to pay more if they perceive some extra benefit.

Take some time to identify and measure your key performance indicators, as they will allow you to monitor the performance of your business and to spot when something is going wrong, enabling you to quickly adjust it. They give you control over your business and allow you to be in the driving seat.

# Chapter 7: Organise Your Cash

*"Happiness is a positive cash flow."*
**Fred Adler**

Cash is oxygen to a business, and profit is the food. The business can cope without profit for a fairly long time, but without cash the business will quickly suffocate.

Cash is vital to pay staff, suppliers and you, so it's important to ensure it's managed carefully. Fortunately there are things you can do to organise cash in your business.

The first is to predict the cash through forecasting – don't wince, this doesn't have to be as painful as it sounds – and the second, is managing the flow of cash to make sure you don't run out of it.

## The Tale of Two Brothers

**John** has real issues with cash. When asked what kept him awake at night, the answer was always that cash was the problem. He simply didn't know if he was going to have enough to pay his team. He didn't worry too much about paying the suppliers; it was the people working for him that he worried about. Having to say to them that there wasn't enough money for them would be his worst nightmare. He could feel the weight of all those mortgages on him.

The problem was compounded by the fact that he didn't know what his profit was. If he knew he was profitable then the cash would have materialised, but he didn't know, month by month if this would be the case.

In addition, he didn't predict cash flow in any way. Sure he had a feel for it, knew roughly what his incomings and outgoings were, but he hadn't got a handle on it, and the not knowing kept him awake at night.

John had the comfort of an overdraft that he had to go into from time to time, but he never seemed to get a handle of when this would be.

Most of John's customers paid on time, but there were a quite a few who were always late. He was only able to chase these late payers sporadically, but because he was so busy doing other things he didn't have time to be consistent. He had asked his bookkeeper to do it, but she didn't like calling people at all, so it didn't get done.

**Stephen**, predictably, had got a handle on the cash. He still worried, because that's the nature of running a small business, but he didn't worry as much.

Stephen runs a cash forecast, a simple tool provided by his accountant that he gets his bookkeepers to complete, which they review together. This forecast is based over the next two months and shows all incomings and outgoings and most importantly the *closing balance each week*.

Stephen also runs a longer-range cash forecast that shows the predicted cash flow over the next year.

These sheets mean Stephen doesn't worry about cash.

Stephen could see in detail if, and when, he might run out of cash in the short, medium and longer term.

Stephen's customers usually paid him on time, but if they didn't, he had a system for chasing debts that was always the same, and always produced the same results.

# Predicting Your Cashflow

Chances are you know what your bank balance is now, and roughly what your outgoings will be in the next couple of weeks, but unless you can accurately predict your cash burn rate, you can't really know what is likely to happen.

The *burn rate of cash* is how fast you are going to use up your existing cash flow, and how fast that will be replaced in the next few weeks.

Predicting this burn rate does not have to be difficult or time consuming. Here are some pointers to help you get started.

### Predicting cash in the short term or predicting cash burn rate

- The prediction of cash should be done every week on a Friday; in order to give you comfort that next week won't be a crisis.

- Regular calculating of cash flow in this way will give you a valuable tool to help manage the business.

- Ideally, you should record the date of outgoings and potential incomings on an aged analysis of cash, with a rolling balance so that you can pinpoint when a problem is likely to arise. At the minimum, you should calculate over a set period, for example, 30 days, or four weeks.

---

 To predict cash you need a spreadsheet, or you can use the free tool that goes along with this book. Just visit **book.theorganisedbusiness.co.uk** to download the *'Cash Tracker'* to help you predict your cash burn rate.

Our tracker is a spreadsheet that presents the next eight weeks of cash movements for your business. The starting position is the bank balance on the Friday night before week one, we then take this balance and add to it all the cash we are likely to receive and deduct all the cash we are likely to pay out over the next week, this gives us the closing balance at the end of week one.

We do the same for the next seven weeks to get our eight-week forecast. The incomings and outgoings are best estimates based on what we know.

As time progresses and we actually reach the end of week one, we compare our actual closing balance in the bank to our forecast and then adjust the forecast for this. The actual bank balance at the end of week one becomes the opening balance of week two.

After week four we reset the whole forecast and start again.

If this sounds a little confusing then I suggest you download the 'Cash Tracker' and read this section again whilst the spreadsheet is open.

If you look at the example tab on the tracker you will find a pre-populated example.

## What if?

Once you have a prediction of your cash, you can simply adjust it to see what would happen if a customer doesn't pay or if you withhold a supplier payment.

Once you have a picture of the potential problems and when these are likely to occur in your mind, you can then react to them.

**There are generally only four things you can do if you have predicted a cash problem**:

- ➲ Negotiate with the bank or other lenders for extra finance.

- ➲ Withhold payment to creditors or yourself.

- ➲ Put more pressure on the debtors into paying sooner.

- ➲ Introduce more money into the business.

However, the sooner you predict a problem, the more time you will have to react. If you do not know that the situation will arise, you cannot do any of these things.

---

### Real Life Example

A few years ago, we implemented this process with one particular client and things generally went well. The predicted cash closing balance was a positive cash flow week on week, until one week the bookkeeper came to me and asked me to review the sheet, because in Week 6 it showed a £50K deficit of cash.

She was convinced this was an error on the sheet, as we had never seen this before. I reviewed the sheet, and there wasn't a mistake, but there was the perfect storm brewing. A lack of incoming cash plus wages, corporation tax and supplier payments due out meant that the business was heading for huge deficit.

We used the sheet to tweak a few supplier payments, adjusted the corporation tax payment for a few weeks (I was confident HMRC would allow this) and reviewed the result. This still left a £20K deficit.

We called the bank manager and discussed an overdraft. When we showed him the cash forecast, he was over the moon because we made his job easy as we not only demonstrated the need for, but also the repayment of the overdraft, making it easy for him to arrange and complete. We asked for a meeting with the director, presented the problem and the solutions, and got the go ahead. We put all this in place four weeks before the issue arose, and when the time came, it was resolved.

*Imagine the alternative if we hadn't predicted the cash flow, got to Week 6 and had to find £50K!*

## Predicting cash in the long term or cash flow forecasting

Cash flow forecasting; the process of predicting cash in the medium to longer term, is a valuable exercise because:

- ✓ It allows you to see when you are likely to have a problem with cash over a longer period than predicting cash burn rate.

- ✓ It will show you how cash-viable your business is, and by how much you are likely to have a problem if at all.

- ✓ By knowing the size and the length of the problem, you can then plan to do something about it.

- ✓ Banks and Lenders will appreciate that you have a handle on things if you that you are predicting problems and can show them the future solution.

The physical production of a cash flow forecast doesn't have to be difficult.

**The key elements are:**

- ➲ An opening bank balance.

- ➲ Cash in – money received from your debtors etc.

- ➲ Cash out – cash paid to creditors etc.

- ➲ Typically a list of overheads is included so you can highlight major outgoings.

- ➲ A closing balance.

This is often produced on a monthly basis to give a rolling figure.

---

 To help you with this section simply download the *'Cash Forecasting Tool' which is available at* **book.theorganisedbusiness.co.uk**

---

It is good practice to update the cash forecast for the actual closing balance, and then have the forecast update for this. This will keep your forecast from getting too far out of kilter.

## Cash Control Systems

So you are now predicting your cash burn rate, and you have even forecasted your cash, but you also need good control to help make sure you smooth out the flow of cash.

We have already seen there are only four things you can do to increase your cash (see page 163).

This section is concerned with the third one; putting pressure on your debtors or customers to pay.

## Credit control

A good credit control system is worth its weight in gold. The system doesn't have to be over-complicated; it simply needs to be systematic and capable of applying increasing pressure on the late paying customers without upsetting the good ones.

*Here is a good start to your system:*

- It is a good idea if this is an individual role so only one person is responsible for it.

- Make sure you have an aged debtors report (a report showing the relative age of each of your outstanding invoices) so you know whom to chase first. Most computerised bookkeeping packages will do this for you.

- Review a list of debtors at the beginning of each week and make a note to which debtors you are going to:

  - Call.

  - Send a statement.

  - Send a letter, which should increase in severity, from the first letter enclosing a statement, to the last letter threatening legal action.

- Record everything you do, on what date, and make a note of all payment promises the debtors make.

- Remember you are entitled to charge interest on overdue debts; so don't be afraid to mention this in the letters.

- As a last resort, contact your solicitor to issue a solicitor's undertaking, to inform the debtor of intended legal action.

**SOFTWARE TIP:** www.*xero.com* is our preferred bookkeeping software, and it has a number of functions that help with credit control. Firstly, it produces statements easily and quickly, which can be emailed directly from the software. This saves a few seconds for each statement. You can keep notes on each contact so you can record the payment promises debtors make.

## I'll see you in court

Be prepared to go to court – don't write off debt easily. After all, this is your money, and if your customer is still trading, then don't be afraid to recover it by any legal means. This means you will need to be prepared to file a small claims court notice. More information on the process can be found here: www.gov.uk, and search for *'make court claim'*

Credit control is often about setting the right mind-set, and there is a danger of falling into the 'not wanting to upset the customer' way of thinking. I have seen this before; where someone doesn't want to ask for money in case future work is jeopardised, but my argument is, do you want future work if the customer isn't paying?

## *Retentions*

Retentions are a peculiar aspect of the construction industry.

*Retention is:*

- A percentage (often 5%) of the amount certified as due to the contractor that is deducted from the amount due and retained by the client.

- The purpose of retention is to ensure that the contractor properly completes the activities required of them under the contract.

If you operate in an industry that has these, then don't forget to collect them. Many big subcontractors simply write off retentions, but if you are a small subcontractor, you cannot afford to do this. Often these retentions aren't due for a year after the completion of the work, but this doesn't mean they aren't morally and legally collectable.

Retentions often work hand in hand with applications for payment; if you are in an affected industry, pay particular attention to the payment terms in any contract you sign. I know of people who have been caught out by some strange payment terms in a contract from a national contractor, and these have caused a lot of worry and anguish over cash flow.

*The basic rule of credit control though is don't give up - collect your money.*

## Supplier's payments control systems

On the flip side, you want to make sure you don't pay too quickly. You should be taking advantage of the payment terms, and possibly the implied payment terms for each supplier.

Creditors will often be quite flexible on payment terms, so make sure you don't pay them too quickly, especially if your debtors aren't paying you. Supplier payments are one of the tools for us to manage cash flow.

Keeping in supplier terms is fine, if cash isn't a problem, it may even be getting you a discount, but if cash is tight, this is the last thing you want.

Try not to upset key suppliers, but if cash is tight, stretch them as far as possible. If you have trouble paying tax, ring HMRC and request an extension. Don't bury your head in the sand with HMRC, as they can, and do use debt collectors, and have the power to shut you down.

## Beware the Bookkeeper

If you have a bookkeeper, and you allow them to make payments, then they are probably paying too quickly. This is because debt and the 'owing people' mind-set is unnatural for us as individuals. Most people hate debt, and rightly so, but for a business, a little debt is no bad thing, in fact, it's essential. So be aware that your bookkeeper isn't viewing your business debt in the wrong way.

## To summarise:

Cash is as vital for your business as oxygen is for you. Without it the business will wither and die.

You need to be predicting and forecasting your cash flow in the short, medium and longer term.

Use the *'Cash Tracker'* and the *'Cash Forecaster'* to do this or create a method of your own.

If you do identify a future cash outage there are only four things you can do:

- ⮑ Negotiate with the bank or other lenders for extra finance.
- ⮑ Withhold payment to creditors or yourself.
- ⮑ Put more pressure on the debtors into paying sooner.
- ⮑ Introduce more money into the business.

Like everything, credit control relies on having a *good system* and making sure it is **followed**.

Finally make sure you don't pay suppliers too quickly!

### Don't just read it, *do it!*

There are three important actions for this chapter:

1. Start predicting cash - Download the tools from the website and use the guidance to start your cash forecast. If you already have a forecast review it against the requirements laid out in this chapter.

2. Review your credit control procedures and make sure they are fit for purpose.

3. Make sure you're not paying your suppliers too quickly.

# Chapter 8: Organise Your Paperwork

*"What you do today, will improve all of your tomorrows."*
**Ralph Marsten**

Many businesses want to achieve the paperless office. No paper means less clutter, reduced waste – which is good for the environment and reduces costs. However, the paperless office has been an unachievable dream for a number of years, mainly because paper seems to simply do it better. I believe that the truly paperless office won't happen, well not in my lifetime anyway. However, you can achieve less paper in the office by thinking how and when you need to print items and for what reason.

## The Tale of Two Brothers

**John** had a nightmare with paper, it was everywhere in his office. Sometimes, even the printer output tray was used for storing it. John knew he had too much, but he couldn't get the time to sort out the important paperwork from the useless.

John did have some systems though; he filed his purchase invoices in date order, and these were marked, posted and paid. The unpaid invoices were kept in a separate file until they were paid.

John also had paper folders for customers, but unfortunately he was very behind on the filing. The filing tray became two filing trays, so instead of looking in the folder for important paperwork, he often had to root through the trays to find it.

One of the issues John struggled with was his referencing. He didn't allocate a reference to individually identify jobs, and therefore, it could be difficult when a customer had several orders in the pipeline.

**Stephen** also had a few issues with paperwork, in that the filing was also a little behind. It was in one tray, but it always seemed to be a low priority and didn't get done. This is probably because the paperwork had already been scanned and saved in the relevant electronic folder, so the physical paper was not really needed. Stephen couldn't bring himself to shred it though, as he got comfort from the paper copy.

Stephen gave everything a job number and a quote number, and he tracked costs in his bookkeeping software against these codes, so he could get an accurate actual cost figure to compare to the estimated costs he based the pricing on.

## The Quest For Less Paper

*There are several tools that will aid you in a quest for less paper:*

- ✓ Email allows documents to be sent to a recipient for review, or to be used for discussion.

- ✓ Dual screens allow the user to view two documents at once. The second screen creates an extended desktop so that documents can be swapped easily between them. In addition to removing the need to print documents, dual screens actually improve the efficiency of analysis and comparison.

- ✓ Scanners are now much quicker and can scan an A4 document in less than five seconds. They can even email this directly as a PDF to you. Gone are the days of the early flatbed scanners that took five minutes to scan each page. Modern scanners also have a feed system, similar to photocopiers, which allow a ream to be scanned consecutively. What's more, scanners these days can use OCR (Optical Character Recognition) to scan documents straight into Microsoft Word or Excel.

✓ Electronic to-do list software, such as *Evernote* and *Wunderlist*, are designed to stop you scribbling on bits of paper and losing them.

✓ Tablets! Before I got my tablet I didn't think I would need one, now I wouldn't be without it. I use it mainly for recording actions agreed in meetings, and these automatically sync with my master to-do list. In the past, they would be lost on bits of paper on my desk. They are also useful for making documents portable so instead of printing them out, the tablet stores them and they can be carried to wherever they are needed.

✓ Cloud-based filing software like *Dropbox, Box.net, Livedrive* etc. (*See Chapter 4 'The Organised Computer'*) allows you all sorts of flexible options for storing electronic files.

✓ Smartphone Apps! There are all kinds of smart phone apps to help cut down on paper use, such as *Genius Scan*; use a smart phone to create PDF scans that can be emailed and *CamCard*; an App to scan in business cards and store the data.

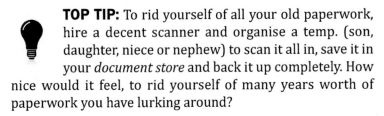 **TOP TIP:** To rid yourself of all your old paperwork, hire a decent scanner and organise a temp. (son, daughter, niece or nephew) to scan it all in, save it in your *document store* and back it up completely. How nice would it feel, to rid yourself of many years worth of paperwork you have lurking around?

## *Organising the paper you do have*

Before you hit the Print button, ask yourself, "Do I really need to print this?" Do you need that item in duplicate? Do you need that file preparing? When was the last time you looked at it?

You must keep all invoices and receipts for a minimum of six years, but it has been accepted recently that electronic copies of paperwork if scanned in legibly and completely, will be acceptable as evidence.

### This is taken form HMRC's website:

HMRC recommend you keep *all the original documents you receive.* This does not mean you need to keep them on paper. Most records can be scanned and kept electronically on a computer or a storage device such as a CD or memory stick.

*Make sure that whatever you use to keep records you:*

✓  Have *both the front and back* of documents so you can easily access them so you can pass them to HMRC

### Sort out your paper filing system

The papers you do have need to be organised. In a small business, it's likely that the majority of your paperwork will be purchase invoices.

If you have to have paper, then my advice is to file these invoices in alphabetical order and then by date.

You will find it much easier to find anything needed that way. Traditionally, filing purchase invoices in date order has been the norm, but trying to gather, for example, all the invoices for a particular supplier on a by-date system is a nightmare. This is because they will be spread throughout the file. Under the A-Z system, they would all be filed under the letter that corresponds to the supplier, and then in date order.

### Don't just read it, *do it!*

Get some A – Z dividers and file all your purchase invoices in this order.

## Customer paper work

Personally, I would scan everything in and ditch the paper, but if you need to keep originals, then I would suggest one paper folder or plastic wallet for each customer, filed in a filing cabinet alphabetically.

### Jobs

If you are in an industry that has job, e.g. specific projects, then it may be worth allocating a unique job reference to the job. This gives you the opportunity to reference every bit of paper and communication with the reference. You can also have a folder on the document store with the job reference on it, to keep electronic files in the same manner.

### Quotes

If you use quotes, then make sure you keep a spreadsheet of everything quoted, then file all the quotes electronically in the customer folder. Don't have a separate folder, either in your paper folder or electronically, for them.

Don't forget there is a *'Quote Tracker'* sheet available for you to download; simply visit **book.theorganisedbusiness.co.uk** and use this to help you with the above suggestions.

### Real Life Example

I recently worked with a client who was trying to organise their paperwork. They had been using a system that had worked for many years, but it wasn't scalable, so as they grew, things became difficult to find.

To start with, they had a separate electronic file for each type of form. The quotes were saved in quotes, the invoices in invoices etc. This meant if they wanted to gather the information for one customer, they had to find the information separately. The first thing we did was implement one folder for each customer so that the quotes, invoices, and drawings etc. were saved together. Next we turned our attention to the purchase invoices, and we alphabetised one year's worth of invoices so that they were all easy to find.

The next issue we needed to address was the referencing system. They didn't have a reference for each job; they used customer location as a reference. This was fine, but as they grew, they began to have two jobs at the same location and it got confusing.

We implemented a job number system – our definition of a job number was a job in one location at a given point in time. That job number was the only unique reference of the work at that point in time. If the job was completed or lost, and the customer came back for a different job, a new number was allocated. We kept an Excel sheet of the job numbers, and the quotes were also numbered and listed on an Excel sheet, so we knew the value of amounts quoted. Each quote had a job number and quote number on it. The customer had a folder, and in it was a job number folder.

This meant as the business grew and we did multiple jobs for existing customers, we knew where all the paperwork was for them.

## To summarise:

You don't need to keep *all* your paperwork, electronic copies are fine.

If you do keep it electronically, make sure you scan the *back and the front of your documents,* and **back up the folder** they are saved to.

Try dual screens on your computers, it will reduce the amount you need to print.

*Try software solutions where you used to use paper:*

- ➲ Evernote.
- ➲ One note.
- ➲ Wunderlist.

Think about how you reference things – could you use a unique job reference instead of the customers name?

# Chapter 9: Organise Yourself

*"Much of the stress that people feel doesn't come from having too much to do. It comes from not finishing what they've started."*
**David Allen**

An organised business is one thing, but believe it or not, the business is a reflection of you. Generally an organised person will have an organised business, and vice versa.

So if your business is not organised then it's because you're not organised. If you're not organised then you probably don't have enough time in the day to finish what you have started and as David Allen, the Author of Getting Things Done, says in the quote above, this is a cause of much stress and anxiety.

The good news is that, among other things, the more *organised your business* and the less reliant it is on you, the *less you have to worry* and the more time you will have.

However, you will still be part of your newly organised business, so you have to become organised yourself, otherwise your business will suffer.

So how do you become organised if you aren't? The answer is – with difficulty. But read on and we will look at some techniques that will help.

## The Tale of Two Brothers

**John** struggled to be organised, and in truth his life was a bit of a mess. It seems his life was full of paper, in his car, on his desk and even in his front room. Every year he got a diary, about the same time each year he joined the gym, and every year he stopped going to the gym and stopped using his diary.

It wasn't as though he didn't see the benefits of using his diary; he just forgot to use it. In addition, he did keep lists of things to do, but he used scraps of paper instead of an electronic list or his diary.

John, therefore, often felt out of control personally, as well as in business, he just couldn't pull it all together. John felt like he needed a personal assistant to follow him around and make a note of everything he said.

The main issue was, that he was so busy fighting the fires his business created, that he didn't have time to be organised. This in itself caused more issues, and it became a spiral.

**Stephen**, on the other hand, used some simple techniques to help get him organised. He had a Tablet PC with Wunderlist loaded on it, and used Google diary for his appointments.

The beauty of Wunderlist was that he could assign actions to his staff, and they in turn could assign actions to him.

The list synced across all his devices and kept him on top of his 'to-do' items.

The diary could also be viewed by anyone who needed it, and having all of this in the Cloud meant whenever he logged in he had the information to hand.

Stephen also disciplined himself to put things in the diary when he agreed them with people, because he knew when he didn't, things were missed.

Stephen also had an agenda for the week, a timetable if you like, of things he needed to achieve each day. During the week he ticked off the achievements as he completed them, and this gave him the comfort that he was achieving all that he needed to do.

*Stephen felt in control of his life and business.*

## How to Start Organising Yourself

The easy win is to get a diary, either electronic or paper, and start filling it in with appointments, birthdays, and contact details. Refer to it regularly to make sure you are where you have said you will be.

The next thing is a *'to-do'* list or lists. As mentioned before, Wunderlist, Evernote or even a paper to-do list. It is essential to fill it out and use it to manage your workload.

David Allen laid out a good system for organising tasks, in his bestselling book *'Getting Things Done'* (this is the model that Graham Allcott uses in his book *The Productivity Ninja* - another great read).

In it, he describes a system for dealing with organising tasks and managing workloads. If you struggle with organisation, or this strategy is new to you, then I highly recommend you get this book and learn the system because it really does help.

In this book you learn to:

- ✓ Capture anything and everything that has your attention and concern.
- ✓ Define actionable things into concrete next steps and successful outcomes.
- ✓ Organise information in the most streamlined way, in appropriate categories, based on how and when you need to access it.

- ✓ Keep current and 'ahead of the game' with appropriately frequent reviews.

- ✓ Keep track of the bigger picture while managing the small details.

- ✓ Make trusted choices about what to do at any given moment.

- ✓ Visit http://www.davidco.com/ for more information.

*These two simple things, a diary and to-do lists will **transform** you life.*

Now that may sound melodramatic, but it really can. How many birthdays or anniversaries have you missed because you haven't put them in your diary? Does you missing your partner's birthday, have a detrimental effect on your life, for example? You bet! A Google diary with all your important dates in it would save a lot of arguments.

## Your day, your week, your month

Another tip is to plan out some micro goals for your day, week and month, ahead of time.

*These goals should link in some way to your overall plan.*

- ➲ Make sure that you do most of the things on the list, and don't let it roll over, if it's necessary to do that, then make sure you complete it!

- ➲ It's quite satisfying to tick off completed items at the end of the week, and this process does jog your memory about items you still need to complete in the future.

If you have set things you need to do each week, then set these up in a timetable format, this will give structure to your day, your week or your month.

### Don't just read it, *do it!*

Previously I mentioned Wunderlist, which is a tool that allows you to set up multiple lists. It is also available as an IOS and Android app. and so can be easily accessed from your mobile device as well. Use it to set up daily, weekly and monthly lists and start using them today!

## Time management

In their book, Kenneth Blanchard *et al.* *'The one minute Manager Meets the Monkey,'* explain a situation where other people in your organisation weigh you down with their responsibilities, or their *'monkeys'.* *"There is a high correlation between self-reliance and morale,"* stress the authors. With humour and logic they describe the delicate business of assigning monkeys to the right masters, and keeping them healthy, i.e. fed and cared for. *"If monkeys are managed properly, you don't have to manage people so much."*

I remember that this book circulated around a few of my clients a few years ago, and one in particular took it to heart. The managers started to recognise what I call upward delegation. The scenario would go like this... Tracy is the manager and John is the team member. John would enter the office and say *"Tracy we have a problem"*, In which Tracy would reply, *"Hmm, do you? John, are you trying to give me a monkey?"*

Everyone in the business recognised that the employees could solve their own issues, but were too quick to ask for help. Eventually the conversation changed; John entered the office and said *"Tracy we have a problem, but I suggest we do this – is that ok"*, In which the reply was *"That sounds good!"*

## The Knock-on Effect of The Organised Business

If you are committed to systemising your business, then the act of systemising and organising the processes in your business will have the knock-on effect of organising you. For example, I no longer have to worry about how to get to my client meetings, as our system states I will be handed a client pack that contains a postcode and a map for the location of the meeting.

### To summarise:

*You are a reflection of your business. If you want an organised business get yourself organised*

- ➲ Try out some different tools such a to-do list and a diary. Try Wunderlist or similar.

- ➲ Set up a diary system and put in all the key dates with reminders.

- ➲ Set yourself some micro goals for the week and come up with an agenda. Possible try a timetable to split up your day.

- ➲ If you find yourself being dragged into other people's issues then encourage them to come to you with a proposed solution.

**Make a commitment to get better organised in your own life. Use the tools I have suggested here or find some of your own but don't be known as the disorganised one anymore. Become legendry for you organisation skills.**

*Remember if you are organised,
your business will be as well.*

# Conclusion

The reason I wrote this book is because I realised that most small business owners are not fulfilling their destinies, and that *not being organised* is a big part of the problem. If you read the section *'About the Author'*, on page 189 you will see that my father didn't really fulfil his business destiny, and that it wasn't because he didn't work hard enough. The reasons are many and varied, and I do not claim that if he followed the advice in this book then he would have, but I think it would have made the journey less stressful and given the business *every opportunity to succeed.*

I wrote this book to help you get the most out of your own business; I wanted to point out some seemingly obvious information, and give you some practical advice on how you can get all your business ducks in a row, to get the most out of your business.

I have come across so many businesses that fail, or fail to achieve their potential because they weren't organised enough.

The most important thing you need to take away from this book, is that you *must not let your business just develop organically*, in a kind of see what happens sort of way. If you want to build a profitable business you have to plan it and then find time to regularly **work on it.**

Plan it by following my advice in *Chapter 2, produce a vision* that you are working towards, and then find time to regularly work on it.

*If the only thing you do, after reading this book, is to work ON your business and develop it's systems and procedures, as outlined in Chapter 3, you will be ahead of 95% of all small businesses.*

Most small businesses do not have a plan that they regularly refer to, and most small business do not have documented systems. Most small businesses fail.

## How Can We Help?

I realise that this book asks a lot of you. It covers a lot of ground and asks you to make some serious changes both personally and to your business.

We can help you in several ways. At various stages throughout this book, I have put some references to our website book.theorganisedbusiness.co.uk and the free tools available on it. Your *free access* will give you all the tools we have discussed in the book, for you to download and use in your business.

There are several levels to the website and for a small annual subscription, you can upgrade to get access to my course which covers all aspects of the book in more detail, and contains webinars, videos and guides on implementing 'The Organised Business' in your business.

We will also invite you along to *The Organised Business Seminars* that we will be running locally which aim to bring experts together and give you fresh ideas to kick-start your business.

Finally, why not hire us to come and run a turnaround session on your business? Simply email me at **will@theorganisedbusiness.co.uk** for more details.

*Oh and one more thing....*

How many times have you read a business book and failed to implement the things you have just read, found it too difficult to understand, or lacked the motivation to make it happen?

Well now is the time, my fellow business owners while the fire is in your belly and the information we have gone though is fresh in your mind. Make a commitment to start and go and work on that business!

*If you always do what you've always done, you'll get what you've always had.*

# About the Author

I am a Chartered Accountant, and own a number of businesses, including Accsys Accountants Limited, a firm of accountants. I am a Franchisor, and own Your Books Online, a franchised bookkeeping business and The Organised Business Ltd.

Right from the start I planned to create businesses with a difference. I wanted businesses that were systemised and didn't rely on their owners. I started with Accsys Accountants. I now realise that an Accountancy Practice is the worst business to set up so that it does not rely on the owner but I like a challenge. My Accountancy firm's biggest USP though isn't its systems, it's that we look at the whole business not just the accounts. Whilst working in these small businesses I have seen that most small businesses suffer with the same issues – caused by a lack of organisation.

I have always been interested in business; in fact I consider my background to be small business. I literally grew up and spent my formative years around my father's sign making business. My playground was his workshop, and the tools of his trade were my toys.

My father was a tradesman and a technician, and like many of the traditional tradesman, saw many of the traditional approaches being made obsolete by technology. Fortunately he loved technology, and once he had bought his first computer, the Apple IIe; he didn't look back.

As most self-employed people are, he was an extremely hard worker, and worked every hour he could to keep his wife and three children fed and clothed. I watched him build his business up to a point where it made him a fairly good living.

Unfortunately, my father's business failed in 1999, and I saw him age ten years overnight because of it. The business failed for many reasons, but mainly because he tried to expand it beyond the point where he could comfortably control it.

His success in the early years couldn't carry on because he had to relinquish some of the control over his business, and he didn't have the mechanisms in place to allow him to comfortably delegate the work. In addition, there was a void of good advice for small business people at the time, so he took on investors, but along with the investment, they gave him bad advice, and this ultimately led to the business closing.

The failure of my father's businesses had a profound effect on the whole family, but mostly him because the business had become such a big part of his life. He lived and breathed and even raised his children in it. Like most small businessmen and women, this business defined a big part of who he was, he sacrificed big chunks of his time to it, and when it was taken away from him it hurt, and it took a long time to get over it.

When I left school, I nearly joined the family business but despite working there in the holidays, and then for a short period post high school I just couldn't find my place in it. The business really was a family operation; it already employed my mum, uncle and two brothers by the time I tried to get involved.

Ultimately I didn't end up working in the business because, maybe I knew deep down that having all your eggs in one basket was a big mistake, or maybe it's because I needed to go out there and bring new ideas back. More than likely, it was that I was bit rubbish at sign making.

Whatever the reason I carried on in education, and went on to take my A levels, then my degree in business and finance, and then qualified as a Chartered Accountant in 2005.

However, because of my childhood, watching my father run his business, my awareness of the sacrifice it takes to make it work, and because I had seen him struggle to make it work, I was never going to be a traditional accountant. Since qualifying, I have always been more interested in the whole business, rather than just the accounts and finance.

I think it's a fair comment to say that in the past, accountants have tended to be perceived as backward-looking and reactive, whilst entrepreneurs as forward thinking and proactive. I decided that I should try to bridge the gap between the accountant and entrepreneur.

Because of my father's business, I developed a need to help businesses owners avoid the anguish my dad felt when his business folded. I wanted to create a better way.

So at Accsys Accountants we set out an offer that includes everything you would get from an existing accountant, but with business advice thrown in

Whilst building Accsys Accountants, I have implemented all the items discussed in this book. What's more, I have implemented them, or elements of them in many small businesses so I know they work. Implementing this isn't going to be easy, but it is essential. Yes, the business can work without it, but we want more, don't we? We want it to be as successful as it can be.

# Reference

*Leadership and the One Minute Manager* - Kenneth Blanchard Patricia Zigarmi & Drea Zigarmi

*The One Minute Manager Meets the Monkey* - Kenneth Blanchard, William Oncken Jr. & Hal Burrows

*The E-Myth Revisited: Why Most Small Businesses Don't Work and What to Do About It* - Micheal E. Gerber

*Work the System: The Simple Mechanics of Making More & Working Less* - Sam Carpenter

*The 7 Powers of Questions: Secrets to Successful Communication in Life and at Work* - Dorothy Leeds

*Getting Things Done: The Art of Stress-Free Productivity* - David Allen

*How to be a Productivity Ninja* - Graham Allcott

*Accounts Demystified* - Anthony Rice

*The Lazy Website Syndrome* - Tony Messer and Pilar Torres Wahlberg

These books are available from all good bookshops.